T0323606

Cambridge Elements ≡

Elements in the Philosophy of Immanuel Kant
edited by
Desmond Hogan
Princeton University
Howard Williams
University of Cardiff
Allen Wood
Indiana University

THE POSTULATE
OF PUBLIC RIGHT

Patrick Capps
University of Bristol Law School
Julian Rivers
University of Bristol Law School

CAMBRIDGE
UNIVERSITY PRESS

Shaftesbury Road, Cambridge CB2 8EA, United Kingdom

One Liberty Plaza, 20th Floor, New York, NY 10006, USA

477 Williamstown Road, Port Melbourne, VIC 3207, Australia

314–321, 3rd Floor, Plot 3, Splendor Forum, Jasola District Centre, New Delhi – 110025, India

103 Penang Road, #05–06/07, Visioncrest Commercial, Singapore 238467

Cambridge University Press is part of Cambridge University Press & Assessment, a department of the University of Cambridge.

We share the University's mission to contribute to society through the pursuit of education, learning and research at the highest international levels of excellence.

www.cambridge.org
Information on this title: www.cambridge.org/9781009532730
DOI: 10.1017/9781009180559

First published 2024

A catalogue record for this publication is available from the British Library

ISBN 978-1-009-53273-0 Hardback
ISBN 978-1-009-18056-6 Paperback
ISSN 2397-9461 (online)
ISSN 2514-3824 (print)

Cambridge University Press & Assessment has no responsibility for the persistence or accuracy of URLs for external or third-party internet websites referred to in this publication and does not guarantee that any content on such websites is, or will remain, accurate or appropriate.

The Postulate of Public Right

Elements in the Philosophy of Immanuel Kant

DOI: 10.1017/9781009180559
First published online: December 2024

Patrick Capps
University of Bristol Law School

Julian Rivers
University of Bristol Law School

Author for correspondence: Patrick Capps, p.capps@bris.ac.uk

Abstract: Kant's main work in the philosophy of law – the *Doctrine of Right* (1797) – is notoriously difficult for modern readers to understand. Kant clearly argues that rightful relations between human beings can only be achieved if we enter into a civil legal condition taking a defined constitutional form. In this Element, we emphasise that Kant considers this claim to be a postulate of practical reason, thus identifying the pure idea of the state as the culmination of his entire practical philosophy. The *Doctrine of Right* makes sense as an attempt to clarify the content of the postulate of public right and constructively interpret existing domestic and international legal arrangements in the light of the noumenal republic it postulates. Properly understood, Kant's postulate of public right is the epistemological foundation of a non-positivist legal theory that remains of central significance to modern legal philosophy and legal doctrinal method.

Keywords: Kant, practical postulates, republicanism, constitutional law, legal philosophy

ISBNs: 9781009532730 (HB), 9781009180566 (PB), 9781009180559 (OC)
ISSNs: 2397-9461 (online), 2514-3824 (print)

Contents

Introduction

In her essay, 'Self-Legislation, Autonomy and the Form of Law', Onora O'Neill notes that '[a]fter two centuries, a close relationship between contemporary would-be Kantian writing and the original texts must be cultivated rather than taken for granted'.[1] She worries that Kantian ethical and political philosophy has suffered a drift towards views that Kant himself would have rejected, but recognises that responding merely by a rigorous textual, contextual and 'custodial'[2] analysis of Kant's work risks losing relevance. It would 'fail to keep Kant's thought alive'.[3] Her solution is to pay particular attention to those parts of his philosophy that still have contemporary resonance and yet that are at particular risk of distortion. We read this as a plea to establish a more productive dialectic between the original text and modern philosophical and practical concerns, from which truths may emerge that are both more authentic and more illuminating. This Element is an analysis of Kant's postulate of public right couched in terms of such a dialectic.

The fruits of our first forays into Kant's practical philosophy can be found in two articles: 'Kant's Concept of International Law' and 'Kant's Concept of Law'.[4] In these works, our exposition tended towards what will be described later in this Element as a moral reading of Kant. That is, we offered a reading that sees him defending a moral argument for law having a particular procedural form and substantive content. Towards the end of our work on 'Kant's Concept of Law', we began to glimpse more interpretative, hermeneutic, aspects of Kant's jurisprudential method. The breakthrough came a little later when we noticed that Kant shifts from talking about a 'principle of public right' in his earlier writings and lectures on law, to using the language of a 'postulate of public right' in the *Doctrine of Right* (1797). It dawned on us that this was no accident, but that it reflected the realisation, set out in full in the *Critique of Practical Reason* (1788), that postulates are not only theoretical, but can also be practical. We then came to see that Kant's project in the *Doctrine of Right* is, in effect, to present a philosophy of law that locates his political writings not only within his practical but also his theoretical philosophy. This led to the current Element, which aims to expose the importance of the *Doctrine of Right* to his entire philosophical project.

Public right is, in Kant's view, more than public law. It is right-made-public, that is, the sum of all legal artifices necessary to realise a rightful condition between human persons, spanning the whole field of law. Those artifices include

---

[1] In O'Neill, *Constructing Authorities*, 121–136, 122.　[2] Ibid., 121.　[3] Ibid.
[4] Capps and Rivers, 'Kant's Concept of International Law'; Capps and Rivers, 'Kant's Concept of Law', 259–294.

many elements of abiding interest to public lawyers. In Section 2 of this Element, we discuss Kant's substantive views on topics such as constitutions, citizenship, judicial power and international law. For Kant, these institutional arrangements allow us to relate to one another in a way that is consistent with our innate right to juridical dignity, which is to say, our fundamental legal status as free, equal, independent, irreproachable and relational human beings. Innate right – the right we are born with – is not a matter of legal artifice, but it informs the content of the law in subtle ways. For example, it establishes burdens of proof within a judicial setting, and it raises the possibility of declaratory relief being provided by the judiciary against the executive branch of government. Generally speaking, however, innate right does not permit substantive review of legislation. With the exception of rare instances of egregious injustice against persons, Kant's constitution is *largely* procedural.

This conclusion is both at odds with much contemporary Kantian constitutional theory, which tends to defend strong versions of judicial review to protect the rights of the autonomous citizen, and – perhaps surprisingly – is closer also to the real practice of judicial review, at least in the United Kingdom. It exemplifies the productivity of a dialectical reading. A similar story can be told about those who take Kant's writings as the inspiration for forms of federal global governance. Kant's actual position is that public right on a global scale is to be attained by a rather loose confederation of republican states. This reading is preferable to those advancing federal global governance in Kant's name, because it is better able to combine political realism and legal idealism in an authentically Kantian manner. Once again, Kant's actual view turns out to be rather closer to current arrangements than one is typically led to believe.

Kant's account of public right thus contains an illuminating substantive constitutional theory. However, what has been overlooked in contemporary Kantian scholarship is the method by which Kant develops his account of public right. This is why this Element commences – in Section 1 – with a discussion of the emergence of Kant's jurisprudential method. At an important and fairly late point in his career, Kant moved from treating legal and political theory as applied moral theory and became much more *interpretative* (as contemporary theorists would call it).

This move occurs when Kant realises that postulates – which are necessary presuppositions for the possibility of knowledge about the world – can also be practical. In the *Critique of Practical Reason*, he discusses familiar examples such as free will, the immortality of the soul and the existence of God. However, in his mature legal philosophy, public right is also described as a practical postulate. The postulate of public right not only tells us what our most basic political obligations are, but also, more radically, what we must postulate (6:313) about right (as a noumenal object, or entity) in order to reveal law-relevant sense data to be genuine instances of law. Pure practical reason requires us to presuppose or assume this ideal object as one to which sense data about law approximates. While it is true that the content of this postulate is something that constitutional and other lawyers ought to bring to reality, factual legal phenomena are already to be understood as an expression of moral requirements bearing on members of a political community. A merely empirical, or positivist, way of conceptualising law is quite inadequate. Such a method renders law no more than a manifestation of psychology and behaviour and not a set of institutional relations that express and realise human freedom.

Section 1 thus emphasises the intellectual context within which Kant worked, not merely to demonstrate the development within Kant's texts and their relation to the thought of his contemporaries, but to show how Kant proposed that moral reason can be properly employed in a dialectical relationship with existing legal texts and forms. Rather than distinguishing sharply between the 'fact' of law and the 'norm' of moral rights and duties, Kant's postulate of public right explains how reason is *consubstantial* with (i.e. standing underneath, behind and within) an external world of normative claims backed by institutional power.[5]

This point is of the highest importance for modern constitutional theory specifically and jurisprudential method more generally. It cuts against commonly held contemporary views of the way in which the constitution works. Such views tend to treat the constitution only as a system of rules issued by those in authority or backed by convention, which are a mere vehicle for the pursuit of policies that – we hope – are compatible with the demands of justice. For Kant, the method of public right flows from an insistence that the constitution is only fully intelligible as an attempt to actualise the substance of public right. The constitution has to be read as the expression of an inescapable idea of how public governance ought to operate. 'Getting Kant right' proves to be inextricably intertwined with the pressing need to get contemporary public law method right as well.[6]

---

[5] Our choice of a theological term to express the relation between the actual and ideal worlds is deliberate: See Kant's reference to *corpus mysticum* (CPR A808/B836).

[6] Some of the arguments in Section 1 were presented at a conference at Radboud University to mark the retirement of Thomas Mertens. We are grateful to the participants for their comments, and to Alan Brudner, Nigel Simmonds, Susan Meld Shell and Howard Williams for their willingness to comment on an earlier draft. The insightful comments of two anonymous reviewers for Cambridge University Press gave us a further welcome opportunity to improve the text of this Element.

1 From Principle to Postulate

1.1 Introduction

Public right is the sum of laws that need to be generally publicised and enforced in order to bring about a rightful condition among human beings (6:311; also TP 8:289 ff.). A condition is rightful, or just, if it is one in which the choice of one person can be united with the choice of every other in accordance with a universal law of freedom. Public right is a condition in which each person is treated as an end in themselves, which is to say as the possessor of an innate right to juridical dignity. Since human beings cannot avoid influencing each other, right must become public in a system of positive law for this condition to be achieved. Each of us is under a categorical moral duty to enter into and submit ourselves to such a system. This duty is a perfect one: we owe it to each other, and we can legitimately coerce each other to comply with it. Right itself demands that it become public in this way, for it is of the essence of practical reason that it be realised by human action in the natural world. The postulate of public right is the claim that real systems of positive law must be understood as expressions of this underlying moral idea (6:307; TPP 8:349). As such, it lies at the nexus not only of moral, political and legal philosophy, but also theoretical philosophy.

Section 2 of this Element is devoted to explaining what Kant thinks the content of public right is. This content, the 'state in idea' or noumenal republic, is what must underlie any coercive system of human relations if it is indeed to count as law. But in this first section, we trace the intellectual context in which the principle of public right emerged in Kant's philosophical reflections, teaching and writing, and how what started out as a *moral* principle became the *epistemological* postulate of his mature legal philosophy.

Although he spent his whole life in Königsberg, a small and relatively insignificant university in what was then East Prussia, Kant was no hermit: he developed his ideas while busily engaged as a university teacher, reading voraciously and enjoying conversation over a good dinner with his friends and acquaintances.[7] He had a sound grasp of contemporary political developments across Europe and its colonies. He admired several aspects of the British constitution, but he also criticised trenchantly British colonial politics. He sympathised with the American revolutionaries and was fascinated by their experiments in statecraft. He wondered whether the relatively open and benign bureaucratic autocracy developed by Frederick II (the 'Great'; ruled 1740–1786) might be

---

[7] The two main biographies are Vorländer, *Immanuel Kant* and Kuehn, *Kant: Eine Biographie.* The English edition of the latter is *Kant: A Biography.*

a rational alternative to republicanism, even as it closed under his nephew, Frederick William II (ruled 1786–1797).[8] Like many others in Germany, he was enthralled by the revolution in France and horrified by its collapse into terror three years later. The conditions under which Kant worked and the political circumstances of his times are the context into which his philosophy was intended to speak. He did not think of his work as abstract armchair philosophising but as a lively contribution to public debate about pressing matters of practical concern. We should read his works in that spirit.

Kant was the first major European philosopher to earn his living as a university teacher.[9] For fifteen years after he had completed his master's dissertation in philosophy in 1755, he earned his living as a private lecturer by teaching a wide variety of courses, from mathematics to anthropology, and even on one occasion the principles of military fortifications. By all accounts, he was a relatively popular teacher: not always easy to understand, but lively and engaging, prone to making interesting digressions, and perfectly willing to offer a critical response to the textbook he was using. In an often-quoted phrase, he made it his aim not to teach his students philosophy but how to philosophise (APL 2:306). When Kant finally became a professor in 1770, his chair was in logic and metaphysics. However, in practice, his elevation to a chair made only a small difference to his teaching activity. Professors were entitled to continue offering courses on a private basis, so long as they fulfilled their basic obligations.

Although law was taught extensively in its own faculty, some elements were also taught in the philosophy faculty, where it was part of practical philosophy. From the foundation in Heidelberg in 1661 of the first German chair in natural law and the law of nations, the influence of the medieval, Aristotelian, tradition had waned, and the teaching of ethics and jurisprudence had become dominated by the modern natural law theory of Hugo Grotius (1583–1645) and his successors. Grotian natural law theory sought to justify the authority of the state and its laws on the basis of an original contract between human beings as possessors of natural rights; his work also included a groundbreaking account of the law of nations. The professors of practical philosophy at Königsberg in Kant's time taught ethics, natural law and the law of nations, and in his private capacity as lecturer, Kant turned his hand to these subjects as well. So, although his salaried chair was in logic and metaphysics, he ended up teaching ethics twenty-eight times from 1756 to 1794. From 1766, he also offered a course in natural law, but this subject was not as popular with students. Kant's classes

---

[8] Clark, *The Iron Kingdom*, 252.
[9] A wealth of background material can be found on Steve Naragon's invaluable website, *Kant in the Classroom*, https://users.manchester.edu/Facstaff/SSNaragon/Kant/Home/Index.htm.

were quite small, and courses were cancelled several times for lack of interest. Nevertheless, he still ended up teaching the subject twelve times, roughly every other year from 1767 to the late 1780s.

Kant lectured from textbooks into the margins of which he scribbled a very large number of tiny, almost illegible, notes. University teachers were required by the Prussian government to adopt an approved textbook, but Kant did not follow these texts slavishly. They were a springboard for his own thoughts. Sometimes he had blank sheets interleaved with the textbook pages to give himself more space for his thoughts. In his contributions to the collected works of Kant, the scholar Erich Adickes sought with great ingenuity to date these notes by reference to such features as the colour of the ink, the handwriting and placement on the page, effectively providing an insight into Kant's intellectual development over time. A few more enterprising students would write up their own lecture notes for printing and circulation among fellow students. Several sets of notes from Kant's lectures on ethics have survived, but, sadly, only one set of notes on natural law is extant (L-NR 27:1317–94). We have to use these texts with caution – they are, after all, student lecture notes – but alongside the textbook annotations they also give us clues as to the development of Kant's thinking.

The fullest statement of Kant's philosophy of public right is to be found in his *Doctrine of Right* (1797), which is itself the first part of the *Metaphysics of Morals*, his last major work of practical philosophy. There is no doubt that the manuscript Kant sent to the printer was disordered and it may also have contained earlier draft material. As a result, the work is disjointed and obscure in places. Moreover, the contents are – to many philosophers' eyes – rather strange. Kant's discussion seems to get mired quickly in obscure elements of Roman law and oddments of late eighteenth-century administrative law and criminal process. How are these supposed to flow from the timeless prescriptions of pure practical reason? If one argument stands out, it is the claim that the duty of obedience to the sovereign is absolute, denying any right of resistance or rebellion. Kant was undeniably respectful of Frederick II's rational autocracy, but any absolute duty of obedience seems directly to contradict the categorical imperative that grounds all duty. How is that supposed to fit together? Kant himself admitted that his intellectual powers were starting to wane – after all, he was 73.[10] Many philosophers have taken him at his word and quietly set the work to one side.[11]

---

[10] See Fenve, *Late Kant*, 1–7.

[11] See Kuehn, *Kant: A Biography* (note 7), 393–8. Arendt considered the *Doctrine of Right* 'pedantic and boring', citing Schopenhauer's view: 'It is as if it were not the work of this great

There can be no doubt about the sorry state of the 1797 manuscript. Kant had wanted to publish a metaphysics of morals for decades,[12] and time was now running out. But close attention to his work as a teacher shows that he had been reflecting on questions of law and government for over forty years. He remarked in 1764 or 1765 that Rousseau had 'set him right' about the value of human freedom (NOFBS 20:43–44). His first intellectual breakthrough in political theory seems to have come in, or shortly after, 1776, several years before his publications in practical philosophy. This was, of course, the year of the American Declaration of Independence and the first colonial experiments in constitutionalism. At this point, he fully articulates the idea that the creation of a certain sort of political order akin to those early American experiments is a matter of moral necessity. Thereafter, he continued to refine his critical philosophy of law up to the point of his death. There is clear evidence of this development in his lectures and teaching materials. The *Doctrine of Right* contains evidence of intellectual refinement relative to the most similar work immediately preceding it, *Toward Perpetual Peace* (1795). Even his posthumous papers contain a paragraph in which he states for the first time the significance of what he had achieved for the practical study of law (OP 21:178). By this stage, the motor for intellectual development had become a second breakthrough: his recognition that the moral principle of public right has a central epistemic role to play in our cognition of legal phenomena. Public right is not merely a moral principle; it is a practical postulate.

When the *Doctrine of Right* is set against the background of this longer-term intellectual development, it looks much less strange.[13] In the rest of this section, we consider in more detail those elements of Kant's thought that are most relevant to the development of the postulate of public right. First, we consider the extent to which his views on public right developed in relation to the theories of earlier political philosophers, focusing on the two he most admired: Thomas Hobbes and Jean-Jacques Rousseau. Then we notice the emergence of a principle of public right in his lectures on ethics and natural law in the 1770s and 1780s. Finally, we set out the steps by which he came to treat public right as a practical postulate, and we explain the significance of this move. It represents his mature and final position.

---

man, but the product of an ordinary common man.' (Arendt, *Lectures on Kant's Political Philosophy*, 7–8).

[12] He stated his intention to do so in a letter to Johann Heinrich Lambert on 31 December 1765 (Corr 10:55–7).

[13] Ludwig has shown that it is possible to reconstruct the text of the *Doctrine of Right* into something much more orderly, but, although attractive, his efforts remain controversial among Kant scholars. Ludwig, *Kants Rechtslehre*; 'Einleitung' in Ludwig, *Immanuel Kant, Metaphysische Anfangsgründe der Rechtslehre*.

1.2 Public Right and Political Theory

After commenting to his students in 1784 that no one had yet realised that our most basic positive moral obligation is to join with others in a system of public right, Kant added, 'Hobbes and Rousseau already had some thoughts about this' (L-NR 27:1337). Jean-Jacques Rousseau (1712–1778) was a great admirer of Thomas Hobbes (1588–1679), and the writings of both political theorists had a significant influence on Kant. This influence should not be taken for granted. In their time, both were radical thinkers whose writings were widely execrated and even banned. In adopting elements of their thought, Kant took the intellectual tradition he had inherited in completely new directions.

That tradition was dominated by the need to solve the religious and political crises that engulfed Europe in the first half of the seventeenth century. The effects of the English civil war (1642–1648) were mild compared to the horrendous brutality and social devastation of the Thirty Years War (1618–1648) on the continental European mainland. Hobbes had responded to the wars of religion by arguing that the psychological inclination and natural right of self-preservation belonging to all human beings should lead them to submit themselves to a sovereign power with overwhelming authority. Since human beings are naturally wary of each other, this is the only way to solve the problem of war. If it is to secure peace, sovereign power must extend even to the control of religious belief and worship. It was this point – the subordination of religion to the needs of the state – together with his evident scepticism about central truths of orthodox Christianity that led to his widespread condemnation.

Kant's intellectual tradition sought to solve the problem of religious and political difference in a diametrically opposed way. Starting with Samuel Pufendorf (1632–1694) and reaching its fullest expression in the work of the polymath Christian Wolff (1679–1754), the natural law thinkers of the German Enlightenment, along with lesser luminaries such as Alexander Gottlieb Baumgarten (1714–1762) and Gottfried Achenwall (1719–1772), sought to identify the duties of reason common to all religion.[14] For the most part conventionally theistic, they argued that through reason God had made known to human beings the rules of right conduct. Law ought to reflect the rule of reason. Its content was a matter of natural right, independent of divine revelation, church authority and confessional difference. One might say that whereas Hobbes sought to solve the problem of religious conflict by suppressing it through an appeal to prudential self-interest, the philosophers of the German Enlightenment sought to transcend it by appeal to a common morality. Such

---

[14] Hochstrasser, *Natural Law Theories in the Early Enlightenment*; Haakonssen, 'German Natural Law', 251–90; Tierney, *Liberty and Law*, 306–54.

thinkers were increasingly optimistic about the possibilities of human perfect-ibility and argued that governments had the duty to bring those they governed into a state of moral perfection. Such theories lent themselves to the legitimisation of more or less benign autocracies.

1.2.1 Kant and Hobbes

In some early reflections on Baumgarten's *Elements of First Practical Philosophy*, Kant set out what puzzled him about Hobbes's arguments.

> Leviathan: the condition of society, which is in accordance with the nature of human beings. According to the rules of security. I can be either in a state of equality and have freedom to be unjust myself and suffer, or in a state of subjection without this freedom ... The social contract, or public right as a ground of the [crossed out: public] supreme power. Leviathan or the supreme power as a ground of public right. (NF 19:99)[15]

Kant seems to be struggling here with a double dilemma. The first aspect is that either human beings are free and each other's equals – in which case we are vulnerable to each other's unjust actions – or we subject ourselves to the power of government. This means subordinating our judgment to that of another, with whom we may well end up disagreeing. Either way, we are not free. The second aspect is that either the social contract is the foundation of supreme power – in which case it is not obvious how it binds us – or supreme power precedes the social contract, in which case it is unlimited by the contract. This was a well-known problem. Other social contract theorists tended to resort to the laws and judgment of God to explain the binding nature of the social contract, but that is a route that neither Hobbes nor Kant wished to take.

As far as Hobbes was concerned, our overwhelming need for self-preservation leads us to give up our natural liberty and submit ourselves to the Leviathan state along with whatever it commands. But Kant does not limit practical reason to questions of prudent self-interest. Quite the opposite: morality is necessarily (but not exclusively) other-regarding. It may well be in the interests of most of us human beings to trade natural freedom for security, but we are not *morally obligated* to do this. We may *desire* peace, but desire is no guide to what is just. So Kant added this thought:

---

[15] There is a puzzle over how much of Hobbes's work Kant had read. Kant did not read English, and *Leviathan* (1651) was not translated into German until 1794. It is generally assumed that like other continental philosophers, he relied on *De Cive* (1642), which was originally written in Latin, and some of his references are clearly to *De Cive*. But as this note shows, at the very least he used the term 'Leviathan' as the label for Hobbes's arguments, and since Hobbes published a Latin edition of his works in 1668, it is possible that Kant had come across the term there.

> The state of nature: Hobbes's ideal. Here the right in the state of nature and
> not the factum is considered. It is to be proved that it would not be arbitrary to
> leave the state of nature, but instead necessary according to the rules of right.
> (NF 19:100)

Kant agreed with Hobbes that the state of nature is one of perpetual war (*bellum omnium in omnes*), at least in the sense that people are insecure and perpetually vulnerable to possible violence. He also agreed that leaving the state of nature is a matter of rational necessity. Hobbes stands for the fundamentally correct proposition: *exeundum esse e(x) statu naturali* (the natural state must be exited) (RBMR 6:97 n).[16] Kant credited Hobbes with being the only political philosopher before himself to recognise that leaving the state of nature is not simply advantageous but rationally unavoidable (Eth-V 27:590). Where he disagreed was over the nature of the necessity at stake. What needs to be proved is that leaving the state of nature is a perfect moral duty, and Kant was correct that Hobbes had not shown that.

Kant gives his fullest treatment of Hobbes's arguments in the second part of his 'Theory and Practice' essay (1793) (TP 8:273–313). Subtitled 'Against Hobbes', he mounts several arguments against Hobbes's position. His opening claim is that a civil constitution is willed by reason itself without regard for any empirical end human beings may happen to have. It is the consequence of freedom in external relations:

> Right is the limitation of the freedom of each to the condition of its harmony
> with the freedom of everyone insofar as this is possible in accordance with
> a universal law; and public right is the sum of external law which makes such
> a thoroughgoing harmony possible. (TP 8:290)

This can be contrasted with any theory that seeks to make happiness the foundation of political order. Kant defines 'happiness' as a catch-all term for any empirical end that human beings might seek to promote through government, such as security or welfare (MM 6:318). Since we disagree about what is conducive to our happiness, it cannot form an adequate basis for a universally valid principle (TP 8:290, 298; Eth-C 27:253–4). The assumption that political authority is necessary to secure 'happiness' leads to instability between two forms of despotism (TP 8:302). Government can become despotic when it acts on the basis of a view of what will make people happy instead of securing their equal freedom to decide on such matters for themselves. The people can become despotic when they rebel against government for failing to act according to their conception of happiness. Kant clearly has Hobbes in mind for the first danger; although he does not say so, he probably has the aftermath of the French Revolution, and behind that, Rousseau's ideas, in mind

---

[16] The Latin phrases – which Kant uses several times – are loose quotations from Hobbes, *De Cive*, 1.12 and 1.13, respectively.

as the opposite problem. The point is that morality for Kant is not fundamentally about happiness but about being worthy of happiness (CPR A806–7/B834–5). Political order must be based on respect for our freedom as human beings, our equality as subjects and our independence as citizens. It is still true that 'public well-being' is the highest object of the law – another Hobbesian claim, which was a commonplace of all contemporary political theory – but what Kant means by that term is universal freedom in conformity with law, not some set of desires or interests (TP 8:298; G 4:447–8; CJ 5:177–8 n1; CPrR 5:25).

Kant also associates Hobbesian empiricism with the error of treating the social contract as a real past event (TP 8:297). In fact, although he wrote at times as if it were an historical event, Hobbes is better read as treating the social contract as a hypothetical thought-experiment necessarily leading us out of the natural state. It is a matter of mere accident whether it ever actually happened. Either way, for Kant the social contract is a pure idea of reason, necessarily presupposed by all political and legal systems, and therefore always relevant as a critical standard. For both Hobbes and Kant, the social contract is sublimated, but whereas for Hobbes it is replaced by the obligation of complete submission to the sovereign, for Kant it becomes a metaphor for subjection to universal rules of law.[17]

1.2.2 Kant and Rousseau

If Kant's relation to Hobbes's work was one of deep respect, in the case of Rousseau it was open admiration, although not without some distaste for the latter's showiness and desire for rhetorical effect.[18] A portrait of Rousseau was apparently the only adornment on the walls of his otherwise bare study. Kant came across Rousseau's works in 1762, the year in which both *Du Contrat Social* and *Emile* were published, and he may even have already read some of Rousseau's earlier writings. Kant credited Rousseau with having set him right on questions of human nature and human virtue, and the story is told of how he broke his otherwise clockwork routine by abandoning his daily walk to devour the newly published *Emile*. Since *Emile* contains a summary of the social contract, and given Kant's reading habits, it seems unlikely that he did not seek to read all of Rousseau's work.[19] As far as he was concerned, Rousseau was the Isaac Newton of the moral world.[20]

---

[17] O'Neill, 'Kant and the Social Contract Tradition', 170–85.

[18] See Vorländer, *Immanuel Kant*, note 7, sections II.2 and II.3.

[19] Vorländer (section IV.4) claims that there is no evidence of the influence of Rousseau's political ideas on Kant's writings before the 1780s, but the notes and reflections from the 1770s are scattered with references to the general will. There is also an early and unusual – but Rousseauian – use of 'public right' to refer to international law as opposed to constitutional law in the mid 1760s. See Kant's note at [E6457] in Baumgarten and Kant, *Baumgarten's Elements of First Practical Philosophy*, 38.

[20] See Kuehn, *Kant: A Biography*, 131–2, 227, 408, 457–458 n.

Rousseau had struggled with the same Hobbesian problem that had vexed Kant: how can government be made compatible with the free will of individuals? Rousseau's solution was that if the wills of each were combined into a general will of all (*volonté generale*), which issued laws, and if all government were simply the application of those laws to individual cases, then people could simultaneously be subject to government and be free. As Rousseau put it in his *Discourse on Political Economy* (1755):

> How can it come about that they obey without anyone commanding, and serve without having a master, all the freer in fact because, under the appearance of subjection, none loses any share of his freedom except what may damage the freedom of another? These miracles are worked by the law. It is to law alone that men owe justice and liberty. This is the salutary means of expressing the will of all, which restores in right the natural equality between men. It is the celestial voice which dictates to every citizen the precepts of public reason, teaching him to act according to the maxims of his own judgement and not to be in contradiction with himself.[21]

For Kant, the implications were game-changing. If all law can be thought of as emanating from the will of everyone, then subjection to government is no longer a matter of relinquishing our freedom in return for security but is instead the only way of simultaneously living socially and being free. And this also means that the problem of the enforceability of the social contract is resolved, since sustaining it becomes an expression of one's own freedom (one can be 'forced to be free'[22]). The Hobbesian dilemma had been solved.

To see the significance of Kant's appropriation of Rousseau, it is helpful to note the extent of Rousseau's departure from the arguments of contemporary political philosophers. A few years earlier, his fellow Genevan, Jean-Jacques Burlamaqui (1694–1748), had produced an account of natural law and politics, which was as popular as it was unoriginal. Burlamaqui argued that states were formed in two stages.[23] First, people exercised their natural rights to form themselves into a body politic. Then they entered into a second contract with a ruler, or rulers, to transfer their power to an individual or group of persons to exercise power on their behalf, thus creating a constitution. Sovereignty was the attribute of the one who had ultimate decision-taking power in a state. It was exercised in various ways (legislation, raising taxes, fighting wars, administering justice, etc.) and could be divided between different bodies. In practice, as for so many social contract theorists, the original contract dropped out of sight,

---

[21] Rousseau, *Discourse on Political Economy*, 10–11. Cited in Cassirer, *Rousseau, Kant, Goethe*, 26.

[22] Rousseau, *The Social Contract*, I.7.viii, 58.

[23] Burlamaqui, *The Principles of Natural and Politic Law* (1747–8). Kant still owned a copy of Burlamaqui vol. I at the time of his death. See Warda, *Immanuel Kant's Bücher*, 41.

since the constitution and political sovereignty were a function of the second contract. The equal freedom of human beings was lost behind the system of government they had – supposedly – all agreed to adopt. The theory of a double contract was a hallmark of the German natural law tradition: Achenwall, whose textbook Kant used, similarly distinguished between the pact of civil union, which made the people collectively sovereign, and the pact of civil subjection, which transferred the exercise of sovereign power to the government.[24]

Reflecting Hobbes, Rousseau rejected all this out of hand. There is only one contract, the one by which all people combine to bring the general will to expression. Sovereignty is the attribute of the general will. For both Hobbes and Rousseau, the common will has to be united in one person or body combining all public power. While Hobbes thought that there was one basic problem (war) and one basic solution (the transfer of all natural liberty to the sovereign in return for self-preservation), by contrast, for Rousseau the problem is a lack of freedom caused by the economic and psychological dependence of each person on the will of others. The solution is the combination of at least part of those wills into one general will. This is institutionalised by legal guarantees of the formal, democratic and material equality of citizens. It is the only possible way in which the condition of societal freedom (strictly: freedom from the will of others, or freedom from 'personal dependence'[25]) is attainable. Legislation is the mode by which the general will is expressed, and the executive branch of government has to be subordinate to the legislative branch, as the particular is subordinate to the general.

Although Kant gladly adopted the idea of a general will from Rousseau, he differed from Rousseau as to its form. Kant identifies several defects in the state of nature. In the context of international order he tends, understandably, and like Hobbes, to emphasise actual violence (TPP 8:354). In the *Doctrine of Right*, he emphasises the absence of a judge (6:312). Other defects of the state of nature are also indicated, and in his fullest account, Kant summarises them in threefold terms: the lack of a legislator to establish what shall count as right, the lack of an overwhelming executive force to coerce obedience and the lack of a judge to resolve disputes over right impartially (Eth-V 27:590). In this summary, we can trace the influence of Locke, Montesquieu and the Anglo-American constitutionalists.[26] The division of powers in turn makes it possible for Kant to conceive of a right of citizens against the state to 'freedom of the pen'. Such

---

24 Achenwall, *Natural Law*, vol. II, §§91 and 98, 138 and 140.

25 See Neuhouser, *Foundations of Hegel's Social Theory*, 55–81.

26 See Locke, *Second Treatises of Government*, 350–353. It is not always easy to prove these influences. For a source-critical approach, see Ossipow, 'Research Note: Kant's Perpetual Peace and Its Hidden Sources: A Textual Approach', 357–89.

a right cannot be enforced against the government, since that would presuppose a coercer above the highest executive power, but it can nonetheless be appealed to and exercised in the face of non-rightful legislative proposals.[27] Ultimately, Kant makes all three powers coordinate in status, logically necessary and interdependent, together expressing the overarching idea of a sovereign omnilateral will.[28]

These differences from Rousseau were the outworking of a more basic difference as to the philosophical status of the general will. Kant accepts Rousseau's view that the civil condition is not to be contrasted with the state of nature in the Hobbesian sense, but rather with social unfreedom. According to Kant, Rousseau considered the civil condition to be an artifice brought to expression by a democratic organ of government. By contrast, Kant thinks that the civil condition is a morally necessary idea of reason. As he himself expresses the difference, 'Rousseau proceeds synthetically and starts with the natural man, I proceed analytically and start with the ethical.'[29] By treating the general will as an idea of reason, Kant opens up the possibility that actual non-democratic forms of government can also be rendered compatible with public right: 'To govern autocratically and yet in a republican way, that is, in the spirit of republicanism and on an analogy with it – that is what makes a nation satisfied with its constitution' (CF 7:86 n).

1.3 From Private to Public Right

As we will see, if the general will is an idea of reason, it becomes possible to conceive of public right as a practical postulate. At first, however, like many of his modern interpreters, Kant thought of it only as a fundamental moral principle. The development of this principle, which is foundational for political and legal order, is evident in his lectures on ethics and law.

1.3.1 The Principle of Public Right in Kant's Lectures on Ethics

Kant taught ethics using Gottlieb Baumgarten's *Elements of First Practical Philosophy* (1760) and *Philosophical Ethics* (1740).[30] He also used other texts by Baumgarten for his lectures on metaphysics. Baumgarten wrote in the dominant philosophical tradition of Christian Wolff, but he moderated Wolff's views in a way that made them more theologically acceptable. Wolff had been accused of fatalism, which implied practical atheism, and as a result he was expelled by the

---

[27] Guyer, '"Hobbes is of the opposite opinion" Kant and Hobbes on the Three Authorities in the State', 91–119, 98, and Fenve, *Late Kant*, 32–46.
[28] See 40–43 for more details.   [29] Vorländer, II.3 (*Rousseau*).
[30] Bacin, 'Kant's Lectures on Ethics and Baumgarten's Moral Philosophy', 15–33.

conservative King Frederick William I of Prussia from his chair at the University of Halle in 1723. He was later reinstated by the more tolerant Frederick II. Baumgarten's pietist upbringing and theological orthodoxy is unlikely to have swayed Kant's decision to use his books, for where Kant departed most clearly from Baumgarten was over the place of God in moral philosophy (e.g. CPrR 5:125–6). Much more significant were the clarity and concision of his writing, and the way in which his ideas moderated the Wolffian ethical tradition in a direction congenial to Kant's own thought. In particular, Baumgarten placed the concept of obligation at the centre of his practical philosophy, displacing a typical concern with happiness and virtue, and he redefined perfection as moral righteousness, rather than in terms of classical *eudaimonia*, or human flourishing. He also redirected attention from the deliberations to reason towards a more subjective concern with human will and intention.

Baumgarten's *Elements* have quite a lot to say about law, but his aim was primarily to create a logical conceptual system of abstract ethical–legal categories such as obligation, right, juridical expert, legislator, court and so on.[31] His book also contains a lengthy discussion of imputation, that is, the attribution of actions to persons and the subsumption of actions under rules. Clearly, all this is relevant to law and legal reasoning, but at no point does Baumgarten use examples from state law. Nor does the book contain any account of the basis of political society or the legitimacy of government and its positive laws. By contrast, in his lectures, Kant shows a much greater awareness of the political dimensions of law. For example, he regularly criticises Baumgarten for failing to draw a clearer distinction between ethical (internally motivated) and juridical (externally coercible) obedience to moral laws (Eth-C 27:272, 280, 299).

In section III of his *Elements* (§§87–99), Baumgarten suggests that the first principles of natural law are that *you shall harm nobody*, that *you shall attribute to each person what is his own* and that in doing so you *live honourably*. This account is entirely conventional; it derives ultimately from a summary of law by the great Roman jurist Ulpian,[32] who himself was influenced by Stoic philosophy. This is why Kant sometimes refers to these three precepts as the *trias praecepta stoica* – the three Stoic precepts. Baumgarten follows Wolff in suggesting that whereas the first precept he mentions (harm nobody) is purely negative, the second is both negative and positive, because attributing to each person what is their own includes both not harming them as well as conferring positive benefits, for example in fulfilment of a contract.[33] The third (living honourably) is simply the result or outcome of the first two.

---

[31] Baumgarten and Kant, *Baumgarten's Elements of First Practical Philosophy*.
[32] *Digest* 1.1.10 (Ulpian); Justinian's *Institutes* (533 CE) at 1.1.3.
[33] Baumgarten, *Baumgarten's Elements of First Practical Philosophy*, §§92–3.

Baumgarten does not tell his readers that he is expounding Ulpian's three maxims, but Kant does, and he always discusses them in their classical order, placing 'live honourably' first. In the lecture notes of Georg Ludwig Collins, he explains them to his students in the following way (Eth-C 27:280–2). The first precept (*live honourably*) is an ethical duty. It is imperfect, owed only to oneself, and cannot be coerced. It is a matter of inner motivation. By contrast, the other two are juridical duties and refer respectively to negative and positive aspects of potential harm. One can harm a person negatively by infringing their rights or positively by failing to give them what is owing to them. Since these two are perfect, juridical, duties, one can be coerced to prevent this happening. Kant stresses the importance of fulfilling one's juridical duty before attempting to fulfil one's ethical duty, commenting wryly on the man who spends his life cheating others and then hopes to placate God on his deathbed by donating his ill-gotten gains to charity (Eth-C 27:282). In all these ways, Kant clarifies, modifies and supplements Baumgarten's account. What Kant has in common with Baumgarten at this point is that both are thinking purely in terms of 'natural' or private law relations between individuals, as indeed did their Roman law predecessors.

Although Collins attended Kant's lectures in the Winter Semester of 1784–1785, they are clearly based on a composite of several earlier sets of lecture notes, revised and amended over time. Modern scholars take them to represent the state of Kant's thought between 1775 and 1784.[34] Collins clearly did not add much to the body of material he inherited, because the notes of another student, C. C. Mrongovius, show us that Kant actually told his students something quite different in the year Collins (supposedly) attended his lectures (Eth-Mr 29:631–3). Once again, the second precept is a purely negative limit of external freedom. We are free up to the point that our actions harm, or infringe on, the equal freedom of others. But now Kant adds that 'juridical laws are really just duties of omission. The whole of law contains merely negative duties' (Eth-Mr 29:632). What Kant means is that a so-called positive duty, for example, to perform your side of a contract, is really a negative duty, since the other party already has a legal right to your performance. Failing to perform a contract is thus no different, conceptually, from assaulting another, since both involve denying the rights of another, whether you do that actively (by hitting them) or passively (by failing to perform the contract). This flips the position of Wolff and Baumgarten in a subtle but important way. Whereas they emphasise the dimension of duty – so that hitting someone is as much a breach of duty as not keeping your promise – Kant

---

[34] Kuehn, 'Collins: Kant's Proto-Critical Position', 51–67, lands on 1775. Schneewind follows Menzer in allocating a timeframe from 1775 to 1784.

emphasises the dimension of rights – so that not keeping your promise infringes the rights of another as much as hitting them.

When it comes to the third precept, Kant now has this to say:

> *Suum cuique tribuere* [give to each what is owing to them]. This is the *jus naturae publicum* [public natural Right], insofar as it is the principle of the possibility of a *status civilis* [civil condition]. It runs: Enter into the state of an external rectitude. In the *status naturae* [natural condition, or state of nature] we have inner laws, but there is no public law or authority there. . . . In the *status naturae*, nobody can determine what is his right or not. So this rule signifies: Enter into that state in which his right can be determined to everyone. . . . The *status naturae* has no public laws, tribunal or authority. (Eth-Mr 29:632)

In other words, by 1784 the third of Ulpian's precepts – give to each person what is owing to them – had become for Kant the first principle of public right.[35] What was once a contrast between negative and positive duty is now a contrast between private and public right. By the time Johann Friedrich Vigilantius was taking notes on his ethics lectures in 1793, Kant can be found explaining clearly to his students the two different ways of distinguishing between Ulpian's second and third precepts: negative versus positive duty, or private versus public right (Eth-V 27:527–8).

It seems that Kant arrived at his principle of public right in the late 1770s. There are very few marginal notes in his copy of this part of Baumgarten's text before 1776, but then several comments dated by Adickes to 1776–1778 contain evidence of his new position. This also confirms the view that the Collins lecture notes depend substantially on earlier material. In the margins of Baumgarten's text, Kant notes that granting security to others for the possession of their rights is 'the duty of civil society, the universal condition of all right and property of human beings'.[36] He continues: 'This is the single affirmative external natural duty: one must leave the natural state: *exeundum e statu naturali*.' In an adjacent note, he writes that giving to each what is their own is the principle of public right, just as 'harm no one' is the principle of private right.[37] And again, he writes, 'The first juridical act in the natural state is the establishment of external justice, i.e. of its form, according to which both right and the manner of rendering to each his own are established validly with respect to everyone.'[38] Hobbes had established the necessity of entering the civil condition; Rousseau

---

[35] Jens Timmermann also notes the contrast between this claim and the subsequent treatment in *Metaphysics of Morals*. See Timmermann, 'Mrongovius II: A Supplement to the Groundwork', 68–83.

[36] Baumgarten, *Baumgarten's Elements of First Practical Philosophy*, 256; [7075].

[37] Ibid., 257; [7078].   [38] Ibid., 259; [7085].

had shown that this was compatible with human freedom; Kant can now argue that it is a matter of perfect moral duty.

1.3.2 The Principle of Public Right in the Lectures on Natural Law

For his lecture course on natural law, Kant chose the third edition (1763) of Gottfried Achenwall's *Natural Law*.[39] This had originated in a collaboration between two professors at the University of Göttingen, the brilliant public lawyer Johann Stephan Pütter (1725–1807) and the political philosopher Gottfried Achenwall (1719–1772).[40] Achenwall's *Natural Law* was an influential restatement of enlightened absolutist thought, and superficially Kant's own *Doctrine of Right* follows its structure rather closely. But Kant relocates its substance within his own philosophical framing, which has a radical effect on its practical implications. Some of the elements of that reworking are already evident in the lectures he gave in the summer semester of 1784 and noted down by Gottfried Feyerabend.[41]

Kant starts his 1784 lectures with an extended introduction that overlaps with the material he uses in his lectures on ethics. This includes a discussion of Ulpian's three precepts, which Kant treats as the main principles of practical philosophy (L-NR 27:1336–7). It is not surprising that his exposition is very similar to that noted down by Mrongovius six months later. Kant also relates the second precept (harm no one) to the Aristotelian concept of commutative justice, and the third (give to each what is owing to them) to distributive justice, since it requires the judgment of a third party to determine a disputed rights claim, and thus to 'distribute' rights (6:267, 297, 303, 306). Nowadays, we tend to think of 'distributive justice' as the set of principles by which legal rights ought to be granted by the state, but to claim, as Kant does, that commutative justice has no effect without distributive justice is simply another way of claiming that rights are insecure outside the civil condition, because there is no one to determine authoritatively the application of general laws to concrete cases. Kant indicates that his interpretation is a novel one: 'That entry into civil society is one of the first duties no one has yet properly seen.' (L-NR 27:1337). At around the same time,

---

[39] Achenwall, *Natural Law: A Translation of the Textbook for Kant's Lectures on Legal and Political Philosophy*.

[40] Stolleis, *Geschichte des öffentlichen Rechts in Deutschland*, Bd. I (1600–1800), 2nd ed., 309–17.

[41] Like many lecturers, Kant ran out of time. The majority of Feyerabend's lecture notes cover volume I of Achenwall's *Natural Law*, meaning that his coverage of family law, public law and international law is much briefer. By contrast, volume II of Kant's copy of Achenwall survived long enough for his marginal notes and reflections to be transcribed in the early twentieth century. Volume I has never been traced, and volume II was then also lost at some point during the Second World War.

a comment to the same effect can also be found in the margins of his copy of Achenwall's textbook.[42]

This leads Kant to reframe Achenwall's material in ways that prefigure the *Doctrine of Right*. Achenwall had drawn a basic distinction between the state of nature and the social condition. Each person has innate, or natural, rights, and the exercise of these rights allows the individual to acquire further rights. This is the context in which Achenwall discusses many of the basic concepts of Roman property and contract law as rational means for the acquisition and transfer of rights. He also considers the enforcement of rights in the natural state by self-help, arbitration, compromise and, ultimately, war. In other words, private rights and private law are simply the result of the exercise by individuals of their natural rights. All this is contrasted with the social condition, brought about when human beings contract with each other to create various societies, such as domestic societies (families), political societies (states) and the international society of states. Achenwall is being entirely conventional in supposing that public law is the result of a contract to establish a certain form of government. Kant, by contrast, expressly rejects Achenwall's basic distinction, replacing it with one between the natural state and the civil condition in which all law is a matter of public, externally enforceable, right (L-NR 27:1338, 1377). The distinction between public and private right no longer refers to the subject matter of law (private law and public law), but to the absence or presence of political institutions to render all rights secure by a system of positive law. The implications can be seen, for example, in his reframing of Achenwall's ideas about the enforcement of rights in the natural state within the context of litigation before a judge.

Kant's final exposition of the *trias praecepta stoica* can be found in the Introduction to the *Doctrine of Right* (6:236–7). Kant gives them a wholly legal gloss. Being an honourable human being now refers to rightful honour – not ethical perfection – that is, 'one's worth as a human being in relation to others' (6:236–7). We can call this a basic principle of juridical dignity. Ulpian's second precept – harming nobody – is explained solely in relation to the obligation to stop associating with others and to shun all society if one wishes to avoid harming them. Since Kant thinks that merely being in the physical proximity of another person without a common will inevitably harms them, this turns the second precept into the claim that the natural condition is inevitably wrongful, and must be abandoned. It is, so to speak, a moral 'push factor' into a condition of public right. And the third precept – giving to each what is owing to them – refers

---

[42] [7937] (1780–1788) Next to J64: 'The first principle of Public Right and external justice is to establish a civil condition.' For a general discussion, see Gregory, 'Kant's *Naturrecht Feyerabend*, Achenwall and the Role of the State', 49–71.

to the obligation to enter a condition in which what belongs to each can be secured by laws guaranteed to all. It is the moral 'pull factor' into the same condition.

From around 1775 to 1797, Kant had been on a long journey from thinking about law in terms of private moral obligations between individuals in a state of nature, to thinking about it as the public guarantee of rights in a morally necessary civil condition. But he was also on a second journey in which he started to think about public right not just as a function of fundamental moral principles but also as a practical postulate.

1.4 Principles and Postulates

As we have just seen, by 1784 Kant was defending a *principle* of public right in his lectures. This was stated as a basic moral duty: 'Enter into that state in which . . . right can be determined to everyone.' This appears to be the end point of Kant's journey exploring the *trias praecepta stoica*, which ultimately concern the implications of the categorical imperative for the state and its positive laws. Put this way, the principle of public right is one of several basic moral principles that are 'at bottom only so many formulae of the very same law' (G 4:436).

At first sight, the *postulate* of public right seems to be no different. It is first mentioned briefly in a side note in *Perpetual Peace*:

> The postulate on which all the following articles are based is that all men who can mutually affect one another must belong to some civil constitution. (TPP 8:349 n)

Then it appears more fully in §42 of *The Doctrine of Right*:

> From private right in the state of nature there proceeds the postulate of public right: when you cannot avoid living side by side with others, you ought to leave that state and proceed with all of them into a rightful condition, that is, a condition of distributive justice. – The reason for this can be explicated analytically from the concept of right in external relations, in contrast with violence. (6:307–8, translation altered)

The claim that the postulate can be 'explicated analytically' from the 'concept of right in external relations' seems to support its derivation from the moral law, as does the normative language in which it is expressed. This has led some to see Kant's principle and postulate as essentially identical, both referring to a moral duty to enter the civil condition.[43] However, this reading is not sufficiently sensitive to Kant's understanding of practical postulates. Although it is often

---

[43] For example, see R Alexy, 'Kant's Non-Positivistic Concept of Law' (2019) 24 *Kantian Review* 497– 512, 502, 503, 509–10 where he uses the language of 'postulate' in the sense of 'Kantian moral demand'.

overlooked, Kant's discovery of practical postulates is a central feature of his practical philosophy, and it is no accident that he uses the word here.

1.4.1 Objects of Practical Reason

Kant had lectured his students on postulates,[44] and indeed their role in practical reason, from the early 1770s onwards (see NL 16:673), but discussion of them emerged in published form in the *Critique of Pure Reason* (1781/1787). In the passages concerning the 'postulates of empirical thinking in general' (CPR A218/B265), Kant explains that our sensations of an external world are governed by synthetic a priori categories such as causation, substance and time. To have theoretical (i.e. broadly, empirical) knowledge, it is necessary to postulate that our sensations do actually correspond to noumenal objects (things-in-themselves) and their relations, spatially and temporally located, and causally interconnected. This, then, allows a distinction to be made between the actual and the noumenal, where the former relates to what we perceive through our senses, and the latter, what lies behind them.[45]

Towards the end of the first critique, Kant argues that there are objects that must also be presupposed as a matter of practical reason, although he does not use the term 'postulate' until the *Groundwork* (G 4:429).[46] In 'The Canon of Pure Reason' (CPR A795–831/B823–53), he identifies three objects that transcend our theoretical knowledge of nature, but that remain the necessary outcome of reason: freedom of the will, immortality of the soul and the existence of God. Although he calls these objects 'ideas', they have 'objective reality' (CPR A808/B836) because they are necessarily grounded in the categorical imperative.

The 'inference that something is … because something ought to happen' (CPR A806/B834) might seem strange at first sight. Kant's argument proceeds by pointing out that although free will remains a puzzle for theoretical reason – and one that he discusses at length in the 'Antinomy of Pure Reason' – it is unproblematic from a practical perspective (CPR A803/B831). Natural causes may lie ultimately behind our wills, but we inescapably experience ourselves as facing up to decisions and making choices that cause effects in the natural world (CPR A802/B830). Whatever medical science may discover, from a practical point of view, we must presuppose that we are free. The other two ideas follow

---

[44] 'A proposition that is provable practically is a problema but a proposition that is unprovable practically is called a *postulatum*' (Log-Bl 24:280).

[45] Waxman, *Kant's Anatomy of the Intelligent Mind*, 532–42; see CPR (A233–4/B286–7) for more details. See also Guyer, *Kant on Freedom, Law and Happiness*, 356–7 and Chignell, 'Belief in Kant', 326–7.

[46] Norman Kemp Smith's translation of the *First Critique* uses the term 'postulate' (e.g. A811/B839, A818/B847), but the German here is *Voraussetzung* (presupposition) not yet *Postulate*.

ultimately from the disjunction between human nature and morality. The problem is that in this life 'happiness', which Kant defines as the satisfaction of desire – an empirical aspect of human nature – does not always follow from moral action, which Kant characterises as 'worthiness of being happy' (CPR A806/B834). In response, he introduces the idea of a 'moral', or 'intelligible', world in which human nature and moral action are brought into harmony (CPR A808/B836). This is the world as it would be if it were in conformity with all moral laws, and it is thus the world that ought to be. It is a world,

> ... abstract[ed] ... from all conditions (ends) and even from all hindrances to morality in it (weakness or impurity of human nature) ... a *corpus mysticum* of the rational beings in it, insofar as their free choice under moral laws has thoroughgoing systematic unity in itself as well as with the freedom of everyone else. (CPR A808/B836)

To describe this world, he adopts Leibniz's term of a 'realm [or kingdom] of grace':

> Leibniz called the world, insofar as in it one attends only to rational beings and their interconnection in accordance with moral laws under the rule of the highest good, the realm of grace, and distinguished it from the realm of nature, where, to be sure, rational beings stand under moral laws but cannot expect any successes for their conduct except in accordance with the course of nature in our sensible world. Thus to regard ourselves as in the realm of grace, where every happiness awaits us as long as we do not ourselves limit our share of it through the unworthiness to be happy, is a practically necessary idea of reason. (CPR A812/B840)

Since ought implies can, this world is a possible one. However, in order for a moral world to be possible, there must be some resolution of the disjunction between human nature and morality. If this disjunction were permanent and insurmountable, morality would be an 'empty figment of the brain' (CPR A812/B840), a breach in the ultimate unity of reason (CPR A815–6/B843–4). Such a resolution can only be achieved if the soul is immortal and there is a God who ultimately disposes justly of all things:

> It is necessary that our entire course of life be subordinated to moral maxims; but it would at the same time be impossible for this to happen if reason did not connect with the moral law, which is a mere idea, an efficient cause which determines for the conduct in accord with this law an outcome precisely corresponding to our highest ends, whether in this or in another life. Thus without a God and a world that is now not visible to us but is hoped for, the majestic ideas of morality are, to be sure, objects of approbation and admiration but not incentives for resolve and realization, because they would not fulfil the whole end that is natural for every rational being and determined a priori and necessarily through the very same pure reason. (CPR A812–3/B840–1)

The idea of a moral world provides an evaluative perspective on the natural world. As he says much earlier on, 'an idea of practical reason can always be actually given *in concreto*, although only in part ... Its execution is always bounded and defective' (CPR A327/B384). The world perceptible to our senses does contain expressions of transcendent practical ideas, but these expressions are always imperfect or incomplete. So the idea of a moral world is prescriptive, motivating us to shape the natural world in its image:

> 'Thus far it is therefore a mere, yet practical, idea, which really can and should have its influence on the sensible world, in order to make it agree as far as possible with this idea' (CPR A807–9/B835–6)

We might assume that in the *Critique of Pure Reason*, Kant's interest in the objects of pure practical reason is primarily theological. Having debunked the notion that the existence of God and immortality of the soul can be *proved* as a matter of theoretical reason (CPR A485–90/B513–8), he reinstates them as necessary moral ideas in answer to the question, 'what may I hope?'. But this is not the only question he is attempting to answer. Kant explains that the question 'what may I hope?' is prefigured by two others: 'what can I know?' and 'what should I do?' (CPR A805/B833). Reason has a speculative interest in answering all three. Kant has already shown that it is possible to have theoretical knowledge of empirical objects. However, reason also has a speculative interest in answering questions beyond the scope of theoretical knowledge, such as 'what is the ultimate cause of nature?' or 'are human beings really (i.e. transcendentally) free?'. The problem is that theoretical reason 'is erected upon the proposition *that the entire speculative use of our reason never reaches further than to objects of possible experience*' (MFNS 4:474). Once detached from theoretical knowledge, further speculation about objects such as God or the moral world becomes inert, and speculation can only lead to idle 'doctrinal beliefs' (CPR A800/B828).[47] Frustratingly, reason requires us to continue to keep seeking answers about objects that lie beyond the bounds of theoretical knowledge.

Nevertheless, Kant ultimately rejects such agnosticism. The question 'what can I know?' can indeed be answered even when theoretical reason runs out; pure practical reason offers something '... from another source, which has not grown on its own land but yet is sufficiently authenticated' (CPrR 5:121). Pure practical reason requires to have 'moral beliefs' that must be held with absolute

---

[47] Thus: 'With reference to my theoretical knowledge of the world, I can produce nothing which necessarily presupposes this thought as a condition of my explanations of the appearances of the world' (CPR A826/B854).

certainty (CPR A828–9/B856–7). These practical ideas re-present events in the natural world in a new light.

Kant's argument for the representative role of practical ideas is an important insight, the form of which has been deployed frequently within social theory.[48] However, Kant is clear that if these ideas are only connected to our contingent interests, they can be denied without contradiction. Since they cannot be grounded in theoretical reason either, they would then float free as mere ideologies. By contrast, once grounded in an unconditional practical principle, the ideas that follow constitute objects of genuine knowledge. This is why the ideas of pure practical reason do not simply answer prescriptive questions ('what ought I to do?'), but also answer the question 'what can I know?'. Negatively, the silence of theoretical reason should not lead us to reject the possibility of knowledge beyond the limits of empirical cognition.

In this way, the manifestations of nature (from external behaviour through to psychological states), which can only be understood by theoretical reason in mechanical terms, become knowable as possible cases of freedom, agency and the divine.

1.4.2 Practical Postulates

Claims to objective knowledge based on practical reason become practical postulates in Kant's later writings. In the *Groundwork* (1784), for the first time, Kant refers to the proposition that other human beings are rational and freely willing as a practical postulate (G 4:429). When, a little later, he comes to justify this claim, he points out that:

> . . . we could not even prove the latter [i.e. the idea of freedom] as something real in ourselves and in human nature; we saw only that we must presuppose it if we want to think of a being as rational and endowed with consciousness of his causality with respect to actions, that is, with a will, and so we find that on just the same grounds we must assign to every being endowed with reason and will this property of determining himself to action under the idea of his freedom. (G 4:448–9 and 4:459)

In other words, free will must be postulated if it is to be possible to have moral duties towards other beings, and for them to have duties towards us. More precisely, we are required to accept that our sensory perceptions of the actions of other beings could be examples of their attempts to exercise free will, and that it makes sense to attribute duties and responsibility to them. In one sense, we

---

[48] See, for example, Marx, 'Difference between the Democritean and Epicurean Philosophy of Nature', 103–5; Kelsen, *Introduction to the Problems of Legal Theory*, 24; Habermas, *Between Facts and Norms*, 106.

could view other humans simply as animals acting under natural impulses, but having become aware of the possibility of free action ourselves by becoming aware of the categorical imperative, we realise that the categorical imperative would not be possible without the existence of other beings with free will.[49] Respect for other human beings, which is, strictly speaking, respect for the operation of the moral law within them, whether they choose to follow it or not, is unavoidable (CPrR 5:76–8). Of course, not every human action is autonomous in the Kantian sense of accordance with the requirements of reason. But human action is rendered *capable of interpretation* as autonomous to the extent that it can be represented as the act of a free and responsible agent. In accordance with this idea, the 'moral world' of the first *Critique* is redescribed as the 'kingdom of ends ... a systematic union of various rational beings through common laws' (G 4:433), or as a 'pure world of understanding as a whole of all intelligences' (G 4:462).

The fullest account of the role of postulates in practical philosophy is contained in the *Critique of Practical Reason* (1788).[50] Here, Kant defines a postulate as

> a *theoretical* proposition, though one not demonstrable as such, insofar as it is attached inseparably to an a priori unconditionally valid *practical* law. (CPrR 5:122)

A little later, picking up on the language of the first *Critique*, he states:

> These postulates [*Postulate*] are not theoretical dogmas but presuppositions [*Voraussetzugen*] having a necessary practical reference and thus, although they do not indeed extend speculative cognition, they give objective reality to the ideas of speculative reason in general (by means of their reference to what is practical) and justify its holding concepts even the possibility of which it could not otherwise presume to affirm. (CPrR 5:132)

As a result, the ideas that are postulated are:

> declared assertorically to be concepts to which real objects belong, because practical reason unavoidably requires the existence of them for the possibility of its object, the highest good, which is absolutely necessary practically, and theoretical reason is thereby justified in assuming them. (CPrR 5:134)

By now, the moral, or intelligible, world, or the kingdom of ends, is also described as the 'best world' (CPrR 5:125), a 'kingdom of morals' (CPrR 5:83) or the

---

[49] '[F]reedom is indeed the *ratio essendi* of the moral law, the moral law is the *ratio cognoscendi* of freedom' (CPrR 5:4 n). For a discussion of this 'reciprocity thesis', see Allison, *Kant's Theory of Freedom and Kant's Conception of Freedom.*

[50] The account is prefigured in WOT (8:141): 'This holding true ... is not inferior in degree to knowing, even though it is completely different from it in kind.'

'kingdom of God' (CPrR 5:137; see also 5:128–30). As a moral idea, it represents an archetype, rendering acts morally intelligible as attempts to strive for it (CPrR 5:83, 129).[51] That is, it becomes another practical postulate.

1.4.3 Postulates of Law

It is against this background that we have to set the references to postulates in the *Doctrine of Right*. The postulate of public right comes at the end of a chain of practical postulates that follow from the categorical imperative: there is free will, there are multiple free agents, a world of free agents is possible, free agents have innate rights, external objects are amenable to rightful choice and we must enter a civil condition. The first two stages – the existence of free will and a world of free agents – have already been postulated as a matter of pure practical reason and are familiar from previous writings. The universal principle of right is immediately redescribed as requiring agents to postulate the conditions under which agential choice is compatible with freedom of all others (6:230–1). Determining what these conditions are is the problem the *Doctrine of Right* aims to solve. Kant then defines innate right as 'freedom (independence from being constrained by another's choice), insofar as it can coexist with the freedom of every other in accordance with a universal law' and traces its implications in terms of the equality, independence, irreproachability and relationality of human beings (6:237–8). Although he does not call the claim that human beings are born with rights a postulate in so many words, he refers to innate right as 'what is internally mine or yours' (6:237–8). As well as pointing backwards to the postulate of the existence of other free agents, this points forwards to the extensive discussion of 'what is externally mine or yours', which occupies Chapter I of the *Doctrine of Right*. This is undoubtedly a postulate (6:246–7); thus, the claim that human beings have innate rights is a clear link in the chain of postulates.

Kant then claims that, 'It is therefore an *a priori* presupposition of practical reason to regard and treat any object of my choice as something which could be objectively mine or yours' (6:249–50). By 'object of choice', he is referring not only to external material objects that are capable of ownership (i.e. property law), but also to our control over the actions of others (i.e. contract law) and our distinctive relationships with others that are akin to property (i.e. family law) (6:247–8). These are the familiar categories of private law. Kant calls this

---

[51] See also CPrR (5:127 n). Kant's view of organised religion and scripture is understood in a similar way. That is, the existence of God *in the world*, as a practical postulate, gives reality to an 'invisible church' to which actual churches are only approximations; scripture should be interpreted as if it expressed the idea of the moral law (see e.g. Rel 6:101). See also Pinkard, *German Philosophy 1760–1860*, 58–65.

presupposition the 'postulate of practical reason with regard to rights'; we could also call it the postulate of private right. Kant's argument is that in order to establish the existence of law at all, we need to establish the possibility of 'intelligible possession' (*possessio noumenon*). This is rightful possession – the only sort of possession we have of an object of choice when it is out of our direct control. The categorical imperative prevents us from willing a world in which intelligible possession is not possible, because to do this would be to deny the possibility that our agency can shape the world around us in accordance with the moral law (6:250). Strictly speaking, even the space within which we exist at any point in time is an 'object of choice'. Intelligible possession has to be possible if we are to possess that space rightfully, let alone all the other things we seek to control. Given that we must also postulate the existence of other agents, intelligible possession has to be possible for all agents.[52] In short, we must postulate that external 'objects of choice' can be 'mine or yours'.

The final step to public right takes the form of a further moral argument. Kant would accept that we should evaluate all acts (including legal acts) by postulating the kingdom of ends. As lawmakers within the kingdom of ends, we are each 'sovereign . . . not subject to the will of any other' (G 4:433–4). This means nothing more than that each of us is capable of determining rationally what moral laws require in any given case. But *acting* as a sovereign in the kingdom of ends presupposes complete independence and access to unlimited resources (G4: 433–4). The moral law does not explain how our capacity to have possession of particular objects of choice can be harmonised with the choices of others in relation to those same objects. If rightful possession is to be at all possible, there must be a way of harmonising the free choice of objects by all agents. In this regard, we are members of, not sovereigns in, the kingdom of ends. The state of nature is thus exposed as inherently wrongful, because even doing nothing in the presence of others is incompatible with our mutual freedom: I occupy space that others may choose to occupy. In a state of nature, it is simply impossible to comply with the categorical imperative. Thus, taking his lead from Rousseau, Kant argues that each of us must recognise that compliance with moral duty can only be achieved by establishing the civil condition, in which we agree on distributive justice, that is, on the authoritative determination of what is 'mine or yours'. Rightful possession in the state of nature can only ever be provisional, 'in anticipation of and preparation for the civil condition' (6:257). In the civil condition, it becomes conclusive. In this way, the *Doctrine of Right* can be seen as the answer to a problem set by the universal principle of right. This principle requires us to will the conditions under which choice and freedom on the part of multiple agents are compatible.

---

[52] Westphal, 'A Kantian Justification of Possession', 89–110.

The postulate of private right provides a provisional account of those conditions; the postulate of public right, the full set.[53]

Part II of the *Doctrine of Right* reveals a crucial methodological twist to this, which the foregoing discussion of practical postulates now makes plain. Just as with all other postulates, sensations about apparent legal phenomena are to be understood as expressions of the ideal institutional arrangements that make possible the just coordination of our choices. Thus, the full implications of the move from the principle to postulate of public right become clear. The state that it describes is taken to exist as an idea of pure practical reason:

> A *state* (*civitas*) is a union of a multitude of human beings under laws of right. Insofar as these are *a priori* necessary as laws, that is, insofar as they follow of themselves from concepts of external right as such (are not statutory), its form is the form of a state as such, that is, of *the state in idea*, as it ought to be in accordance with pure principles of right. This idea serves as a norm (*norma*) for every actual union into a commonwealth (hence serves as a norm for its internal constitution). (6:313)

By the same logic, perpetual peace – which combines state, international and cosmopolitan constitutions – is also postulated practically (TPP 8:349 n). Pure practical reason requires us to postulate the 'objective reality' of an entire public world system of law and legal institutions.

Like the other practical postulates, the postulates of law do not add to theoretical knowledge as such, but they provide a necessary aspect under which the world of human action is to be characterised legally. From this perspective, external objects can take on the legal attribute 'belonging to X' – an attribute that has no effect on their material substance, but must be taken to be analogous to theoretical knowledge nonetheless. In the same way, human commands and sanctions, which from an empirical perspective remain mere coercive events in the natural world, take on the legal attribute of exercises of lawful power. Just as the need to presuppose the possibility of a moral world led to the necessity of postulating the existence of God, so the need to presuppose the possibility of a legal world (a world in which external objects of choice are amenable conclusively to the attributes 'mine' and 'yours') leads to the necessity of postulating the existence of the state within a global legal order.[54]

---

[53] The best summary of the arc of his argument is found in 'Religion Within the Boundaries of Mere Reason': 'Now if the community to be founded is to be a juridical one, the mass of people joining in a union must itself be the lawgiver (of constitutional laws), because legislation proceeds from the principle of limiting the freedom of each to the conditions under which it can coexist with the freedom of everyone else, in conformity with a universal law, and the universal will thus establishes an external legal constraint' (6:99).

[54] Kant draws an express parallel between the moral attributes of God and the three powers of the state in *Critique of Practical Reason* (5:131 n).

Kant's legal philosophy is not, then, merely a moral argument to justify the state and its constitution. The postulate of public right is not merely: 'you must enter a condition of public rightfulness'. Rather, it is 'because you must enter a condition of public rightfulness the state must exist as an idea re-presenting and illuminating the circumstances you find yourself in'. Understood this way, the categorical imperative leads us to a set of necessary ideas, which in turn open up 'a whole field of practical cognition' (6:225).

1.5 Conclusion

Kant concludes, then, that the object of the postulate of public right is the 'state in idea'. This idea is necessarily presupposed by pure practical reason. It is clear that it does not simply answer the question, 'what should I do?' but also the question, 'what can I know?'. As with all the practical postulates, it adds a new layer of our knowledge of the world beyond what can be determined theoretically. Practical postulates interpolate the full implications of our awareness of existence of human agency into our knowledge of the world. Specifically, the postulates of law transform observed behaviour and psychological states into duty, ownership, contract, law, government and legal process in the relations between agents and the material world. From this perspective, a philosophy of law that is grounded only in the empirical is impoverished and inert. Theoretical reason on its own can establish 'what the laws in a certain place and at a certain time say or have said' (6:229) and no more. But, 'Like the wooden head in Phaedrus's fable, a merely empirical doctrine of right is a head that may be beautiful but unfortunately it has no brain' (6:230).

The 'brain' that Kant misses is the postulate of public right, which animates the acts or texts associated with law and allows them to be reconstrued – rendered intelligible – as manifestations of a corresponding underlying idea. Kant expresses this position in particularly strident terms near the beginning of the *Doctrine of Virtue*:

> People who are accustomed merely to explanations by natural sciences will not get into their heads the categorical imperative from which these laws [i.e. moral laws] proceed dictatorially, even though they feel themselves compelled irresistibly by it. Being unable to explain what lies entirely beyond that sphere (freedom of choice), however exalting is this very prerogative of the human being, his capacity for such an idea, they are stirred by the proud claims of speculative reason, which makes its power so strongly felt in other fields, to band together in a general call to arms, as it were, to defend the omnipotence of theoretical reason. And so now, and perhaps for a while

longer, they assail the moral concept of freedom and, wherever possible, make it suspect; but in the end they must give way. (6:378)

Thus, when Kant describes reason alone as the 'basis for any *possible* giving of positive laws' (6:230), he does not simply mean the basis for any *morally permissible* lawgiving. Without the ability to cognise laws as expressions of the idea of a state, the deliverances of a would-be legislator would not constitute acts of lawgiving at all.

2 Law in Light of the Noumenal Republic

2.1 Introduction

Kant's main treatment of public right can be found in the second part of the *Doctrine of Right*. However, any interpreter of this text faces several difficulties. Kant himself warns us that these sections are less developed, in part because their content can be inferred, and in part because they are still subject to public discussion (6:209). In addition to this, the text in §§41–52 of the *Doctrine of Right* ('the right of a state') is almost certainly disordered.[55] Some assistance may be derived from his earlier writings on public right, yet these add another layer of complexity, since Kant's views continued to develop even at this late period of his life. We cannot always know when we are to strive for overall coherence or accept a degree of progression.

However, the biggest challenge facing the modern interpreter of the *Doctrine of Right* is the sheer variety and detail of the legal material Kant includes. Kant himself tells us that we are to observe the distinction between 'metaphysics' and the 'empirical application of rights' (6:205–6). He distinguishes between rights that belong to the a priori system of principles and rights that are taken from particular cases of experience. He tells us that he has put the latter into 'remarks, which will sometimes be extensive'. The *Doctrine of Right* contains one such extensive remark: a General Remark towards the end of the section on the right of a state, which covers a wide range of topics including resistance and revolution, public ownership of land, the nobility and clergy, taxation, welfare, public worship, public offices, crime, punishment and mercy. Numerous other topics and examples are scattered throughout the work.

How we make sense of this material depends on our basic interpretative stance. The literature tends to land on one of two positions, neither of which fully captures Kant's method. One straightforward approach treats the *Doctrine*

---

[55] In contrast to standard editions, Bernd Ludwig argues that section 1 of Public Right ('The Right of a State') only begins in §45, and that §§41–4 form an introductory bridge to Public Right. Whether or not he is correct as a matter of historical reconstruction, this clarifies Kant's argument considerably. Ludwig also reorders the material within §§45–52.

of Right as an exercise in applied moral philosophy, providing an account of the ideal purpose and content of law. It offers an external standard of evaluation for any real system of positive law. By implication, positive law itself is to be treated as a very complex set of facts about human behaviours and intentions. To understand Kant's work as an exercise in critical moral philosophy thus raises no inconsistencies with analytical positivist legal philosophy. The inquiries respond to different questions.

This said, in practice, it is difficult to keep law and morality in watertight compartments, and impossible when attempting to conceptualise the perspective of an 'insider' to a legal system such as a judge. If a judge were to apply Kant's moral philosophy, the assumed separation of law and morality can flip rather easily into a simple or 'strong' natural law position: positive law that fails to satisfy its underlying moral purpose has to be treated by the judge as invalid.

An important second alternative position, and one that can claim greater fidelity to Kant's thought, is to read him as a normative positivist. This treats him as offering an account of political obligation that legitimises whatever laws happen to be enacted by the sovereign. Fidelity to positive law, regardless of its content, then becomes a matter of overriding moral obligation.

The range and instability of such interpretations are striking, and the postulate of public right shows their inadequacy. Kant is not a legal positivist in either its analytical or normative versions; nor is he a strong natural law theorist. Rather, he is making the more complex epistemological claim that legal phenomena must – as a matter of moral necessity – be construed as imperfect expressions of public right understood as an idea lying behind these phenomena. In this section, we review these main interpretative positions adopted by modern commentators before showing how the postulate of public right points towards a more complex reconstructive method. This then allows us to outline a more satisfactory reading of Kant's discussion of the substance of public right, which moves him away from positivist readings towards (what would now be called) a form of non-positivist interpretivism.

2.2 Three Interpretations of the *Doctrine of Right*

2.2.1 The 'Moral Reading'

Mark Murphy uses the term 'moral reading' to characterise one typical modern appropriation of the long tradition of natural law theory of which Kant was part.[56] Although 'excruciatingly uninteresting', moral readings are an intuitively attractive way of resolving the evident tension between our best account

---

[56] Murphy, *Natural Law in Jurisprudence and Politics*, 8–10.

of the requirements of justice, which bears upon us as a matter of moral necessity, and the contingent content of the laws we find ourselves governed by. Moral readings can be traced to the founding assumptions of the legal positivist John Austin (1790–1859) who distinguished between the science of law (law as it is) and the science of legislation (law as it ought to be).[57] This is the distinction between an analytical or empirical inquiry into the nature and content of positive law, now seen as a complex social phenomenon, and the moral question of whether positive law deserves our obedience and respect: 'The existence of law is one thing, its merit or demerit is another.'[58] Even though positive law uses terms that are drawn from morality ('right', 'obligation', etc.), those terms are only to be understood 'as if' they were normatively binding. They are used by legal actors in a 'detached' way.[59] In the view of its proponents, moral readings of the natural law tradition allow us to preserve it as a theory of the proper purpose and content of law while purging it of more controversial claims about the moral necessity and validity of positive law.

Kant makes a number of claims which indicate that he could be read in this way.[60] He distinguishes 'positive laws', which are not binding without 'external lawgiving', from 'natural laws' (6:224). In a similar fashion, he divides right into 'natural right, which rests only on a priori principles, and positive (statutory) right, which proceeds from the will of the legislator' (6:237). Consistently with this distinction, he accepts the existence of permissive natural laws, which create moral options for human beings, which human laws may then restrict as a matter of moral indifference.[61] He further distinguishes 'juridical' from 'ethical' lawgiving (6:218). This distinction is not entirely easy to pin down, but his most consistent explanation is based on the claim that all 'lawgiving' contains two elements: 'first, a law, which represents an action that is to be done as objectively necessary' and 'second, an incentive, which connects a ground

---

[57] Austin, *The Province of Jurisprudence Determined*, Lecture V, 112–13.   [58] Ibid., 157.

[59] Raz, 'The Purity of the Pure Theory', 442–59. See also Hart, *The Concept of Law*, 1–17; and Kramer, *In Defence of Legal Positivism*, 78–112. A parallel debate takes place over the ontological status of Kant's metaphysics; see Rauscher, *Naturalism and Realism in Kant's Ethics*.

[60] For a good, if brief, discussion of the moral reading of the *Doctrine of Right*, see John Ladd's introduction to Kant, *Metaphysical Elements of Justice*. Here, he writes: 'Legal positivists . . . are quick to point out that the practical effect of identifying law with a part of morals is either to nullify existing law in favor of an ideal law, or to elevate all existing law to the status of what is moral; in other words, the natural-law theorist, they maintain, has to be either a radical revolutionary or an unregenerate reactionary.' His view is firmly that Kant is a natural lawyer, but neither of the above.

[61] Preliminary notes to *The Doctrine of Virtue* (23:385): '*Lex permissiva* is the law by which something is permitted by natural law that is forbidden by civil law' (cited in Tierney, *Liberty and Law*, 330). Here, Kant gives examples of avenging injuries oneself, taking more than one wife when men are scarce, and stealing to prevent starvation. For other instances, see (6:247, 267) and Capps and Rivers 'Kant's Concept of Law', 273–5 for a discussion.

for determining choice to this action subjectively with the representation of the law'. Lawgiving can be distinguished in respect to the incentive: 'lawgiving which makes an action a duty and also makes this duty the incentive is ethical' (6:219). And then 'lawgiving which does not include the incentive of duty in the law and so admits an incentive other than the idea of duty itself is juridical'. These other incentives are 'pathological', by which Kant means that they appeal to our fears and desires. The legality of an action from a juridical perspective is merely its conformity to what is required, regardless of the incentive, which may well be fear of enforcement. It is a hallmark of analytical legal positivism, and hence of tendencies to adopt moral readings of natural law theory, to accept that, as a matter of sociological fact, people can be motivated to follow the law for a range of reasons that may or may not include moral ones. The conclusion sometimes drawn is that Kant is happy to conceive of law as a functioning social system independently of moral evaluation. On this account, the term 'postulate' is treated as synonymous with a moral demand, requirement or principle, and the rather lengthy discussions of contemporary Prussian and Roman law must be intended to describe objects for critical evaluation.

The assumption that the *Doctrine of Right* is an exercise in moral philosophy as applied to questions of the proper content of law has dominated legal theory, especially in North American circles.[62] It is, in good measure, part of the legacy of John Rawls. It has given rise to a significant body of work grounded in Kant's ideas, more or less responsive to his actual texts, but typically dominated by the *Groundwork*, which is developed into new rational constructions and then deployed critically to analyse aspects of modern substantive law.[63] For many scholars, this is what 'Kantian legal philosophy' is.

However, those who take the moral reading are forced to admit that the *Doctrine of Right* is rushed, unfocused and a bewildering failure. Whatever the political and personal reasons for such failure might be,[64] we are left with the uncomfortable conclusion that the work is simply of poor quality. A particularly strident articulation of this view comes from Stuart M. Brown in an essay published in 1962.[65] Brown's reading of Kant is based on an interpretation of the passage in which the latter argues that positive law (as identified by the jurist) must be morally evaluated according to 'reason alone'.[66] For Brown, Kant 'would provide us with an account of justice which enables us to distinguish clearly between good and bad laws, between law as it is and law

---

[62] See Waldron, 'Kant's Legal Positivism', 1535–36, 1542ff.

[63] See, for example, the symposium in (1987) 87(3) *Columbia Law Review* 419–591.

[64] See 6–7.   [65] Brown, 'Has Kant a Philosophy of Law', 33–48.

[66] This is Mary Gregor's translation of *blosse Vernunft* (6:230).

as it ought to be'.[67] But if that is the nature of Kant's project, then Brown draws the logical conclusion: his work must count as a dismal failure.

> Instead of showing how the Categorical Imperative may be applied to test the rules of positive law, Kant introduces a number of different principles which range in degree of generality between the extremes of the Categorical Imperative and the rules of positive law. Many of these principles have no discernible logical relationship to the Categorical Imperative and no clear application to positive law. Some of these principles show Kant at his worst, almost incredibly lacking in moral sensibility; others show him at his best, committed to the ideals of freedom and world peace. But there is no consistency in the pattern, no one set of principles regulating the discussion.[68]

The growing gap between Kant's own work and modern applied moral philosophy noted in the introduction to this Element is due at least in part to embarrassment that the great philosopher should have made such a bad job of his own project.

Not only does the moral reading fail to make much sense of the *Doctrine of Right* as a text, it is also deeply problematic from an internal Kantian perspective.[69] If taken seriously, it would follow that those subject to positive law only have a moral duty to comply when the content of law is consistent with the categorical imperative and whatever further requirements flow from it. This would imply strong forms of judicial review, since there must be absolute moral limits on the positive laws judges ought to be willing to apply – a view congenial enough to a North American audience. But, logically, the moral reading takes us much further. It would require every legal official and every citizen to exercise independent moral judgment over the law. In other words, if Kant were only engaged in an exercise in applied moral philosophy, we would expect him to be a strong natural lawyer, even a philosophical anarchist.[70] The categorical imperative seems to leave him with no alternative. Moral readings of the natural law tradition are vulnerable to flipping over into radical positions, above all for Kant, who takes moral obligation with such seriousness.

But this is impossible to square with the authoritarian stance that Kant often adopts, and that appears at the heart of his political philosophy. As seen in Section 1, Kant explains that human beings have a categorical moral obligation to leave the condition of nature and enter into a system expressing and enforcing public right. From this, there follows another categorical moral obligation to remain in such a condition, imperfect though it may be. He insists that citizens

---

[67] See Brown, note 65.   [68] See note 65.   [69] See Waldron, note 62, 1541–1545.

[70] The potential of natural rights theories to lead to anarchy is classically expressed in Jeremy Bentham, 'Nonsense upon Stilts or Pandora's Box Opened'; see also Raz, *The Authority of Law*, 2–27.

may have to put up with even 'an unbearable abuse of supreme authority' (6:320) and obey the law. How can this be reconciled with a strong assertion of independent moral judgment on the part of each individual person?

As we explored in Section 1, from the *Critique of Pure Reason* onwards, Kant understands that our capacity for reasoned choice implies the postulate of the 'moral world' containing other willing beings, freedom of the will and moral responsibility. This postulate makes possible a moral evaluation of sense data, including law-like phenomena. It endorses a moral reading of sorts: we *can* morally evaluate the content of law, just as we can morally evaluate any human action or intention. This is one legitimate way of responding to legal phenomena, one that uses *principles* of right as standards of moral evaluation. But it was not intended to be the subject matter of the *Doctrine of Right*. As we have seen, this work concerns how the social phenomenon of law resolves the Rousseauian problem of the possibility of freedom of choice by each of us as embodied agents given the exercise of choice by other similar agents. Law in the *Doctrine of Right* is not simply an object of moral evaluation; it has to be seen as the necessary consequence and expression of our moral obligations. Kant consistently took the view that practical postulates are not moral principles but instead articulate an epistemological claim based on moral principles affecting how we construe, or interpret, legal phenomena. A strict distinction between 'law as it is' and 'law as it ought to be' is misplaced for this reason.

2.2.2 *The* Doctrine of Right *as Normative Positivism*

Kant's shift in orientation towards the moral significance of the phenomenon of positive law has led some commentators, such as Jeremy Waldron, to move away from moral readings and suggest that the interpretative key to his work is some version of normative or political positivism instead. Treating Kant as a normative positivist takes his legal theory closer to that of Hobbes.[71] For Waldron, the core of the *Doctrine of Right* is the argument that the coordination problems that emerge from divergent desires and interpretations of what morality requires necessitates the establishment of a univocal legislative will. The moral duty to leave the state of nature (6:307) generates a corresponding moral duty to comply with legislation that emerges from institutions in the civil condition.

Reading Kant as a normative positivist is consistent with a modern trend in the history of legal philosophy that seeks to reverse a tendency to describe older legal positivists as if they were part of a single analytical tradition. A contested figure in this debate is Kant's English contemporary, Jeremy

---

[71] Waldron, note 62, 1540–1541.

Bentham (1748–1832). Bentham distinguishes 'inquisitorial' from 'censorial' jurisprudence, and in the hands of his admiring disciple John Austin, this became a version of the moral reading. H. L. A. Hart adopted Austin's reading, rendering the former as an empirical or analytical inquiry, and the latter a moral inquiry into its proper content. Hart then writes that the 'healthy centre' of Bentham's legal philosophy is its neutral and descriptive positivism (i.e. the command theory of law), while the moral evaluation of the law (i.e. his utilitarianism) 'gets in the way of his analytical vision'.[72]

It is now clear that the problem is less with Bentham's jurisprudence, and more with the moral reading assumed by Austin, Hart and others. According to Gerald Postema, Bentham's defence of expositorial jurisprudence is not intended to be an analytical claim.[73] Rather, it emerges from a Hobbesian critique of the obscurantism he associated with the common law and classical natural law theory. His defence of the command theory of law was justified *morally* on utilitarian grounds: there was a weighty 'expectation utility' inherent in law taking the form of clear and publicly known commands.[74] Put the other way around, if the content and application of the law is potentially qualified by common law or natural law principles, then it ceases to be a reliable guide to conduct, and fails to provide a stable system of rules to govern interpersonal relations. It fails to treat those subject to the law as responsible persons participating in social and political life. Bentham's central motivation underlying the distinction between 'expositorial' and 'censorial' jurisprudence was to show how a system of general laws could be authoritative given his theory of *subjective* practical reason (i.e. the principle of utility). It was not straightforwardly a descriptive, or factual, exposition of legal phenomena as a moral reading of Bentham would have it.

Would Kant benefit from a similar rehabilitation? Certainly, there are passages in the *Doctrine of Right* and elsewhere in which he appears to come close to Hobbes (6:257, 312, 354; see also UNH 8:25–6 and CB 8:115). While he must reject instrumental, prudential and pragmatic reasons for leaving the state of nature and submitting oneself to a sovereign authority, he has been read as offering a parallel moral account. On this assumption, each person has a moral duty, derived from the categorical imperative, to

> leave the state of nature, in which each follows its own judgment, unite itself with all others (with whom it cannot avoid interacting), subject oneself to public lawful external coercion, and enter into a condition in which what is to be recognized as belonging to it is determined by law and

---

[72] Hart, *Essays on Bentham*, 162–192, 162.
[73] Postema, *Bentham and the Common Law Tradition*, 302–336.   [74] Ibid., 154.

is allotted to it by adequate power (not its own but an external power). (6:312 translation altered)

This seems to leave the content of law open to whatever the system of coercion harmonised by general or omnilateral willing may determine.

Normative positivism is the tendency of several German commentators who stress the autonomy of Kant's concept of the juridical. We can see this tendency at work already in Kelsen's 'neo-Kantian' theory of law, which combines a view of law as a coercive hierarchy of norms with an insistence that the normativity of law is merely hypothetical. It is only the morally detached quality of this perspective that prevents it from being authoritarian. By taking this step, Kelsen comes closer to analytical than normative positivism.[75] Robert Alexy, who reads Kant as a normative positivist with authoritarian tendencies, sees Kelsen as preferable for just this reason.[76] To take another example, Marcus Willaschek argues that the *Doctrine of Right* betrays an incomplete supplanting of an 'original' view that treats law (right) as a branch of morality alongside virtue by an 'alternative' view that treats law as an independent expression of human autonomy akin to, but distinct from, moral obligation. This allows him to solve tensions in Kant's scheme of moral duties by distinguishing carefully between duties of right (the domain of the juridical) and moral duties to others.[77] On such accounts, the moral element in Kant's discussion of law is split into two: an aspirational dimension consisting of ideals of just governance and an obligatory dimension of obedience to whatever current system of government is in place.

Normative positivist readings are right to observe the shift in focus in Kant's legal philosophy from resources for the moral evaluation of law to establishing the conditions under which one person's freedom of choice can coexist with that of others. The former inquiry requires willing beings to postulate the 'moral world'; the latter inquiry requires a theory of political authority to solve the coordination problems that emerge from freedom of choice. But although this reading is correct to highlight Kant's concern with the moral necessity of political institutions, it seems unlikely that Kant would have landed on a model of Hobbesian authoritarianism. At root, the problem with this interpretation is that it sits uneasily with the foundation of the Kantian system of law in innate (i.e. natural) right. Normative positivist readings of Kant recognise the need to coordinate freedom through political authority but conclude that there are overriding moral reasons to obey any dominating rule system. Thus, they

---

[75] For example, see Kelsen, *Introduction to the Problems of Legal Theory.*

[76] Alexy, *The Argument from Injustice*, 121.

[77] Willaschek, 'Why the Doctrine of Right Does Not Belong in the Metaphysics of Morals', 225–6.

attempt to solve the problem raised by innate right in the natural condition by leaving open the possibility of systems of government that violate it. We might say that normative positivism adopts the postulate of *positive* right: whatever can coerce us is rightful. When Kant discusses law in the *Doctrine of Right*, he is surely saying something more than this.

One solution to this tension within Kant's thought is to give his normative positivism a Lockean gloss in which the exercise of sovereign authority is disciplined by distinct and separate constitutional powers. Along this line, for Ripstein, Kant's project is about the moral justification of state institutions.[78] He regards the three powers that form the state as means to solve defects of the state of nature, which are morally problematic given the existence of innate right. Thus, the legislature provides omnilateral authorisation for what would otherwise be wrongful unilateral acts of interference with the independence of others (the problem of unilateral judgment); executive power provides assurance that all will comply with respect for rights (the problem of mutual assurance); the judicial power provides definitive and determinate judgments about the application of law to concrete cases (the indeterminacy problem). This gets closer to the heart of Kant's project, but has the tendency to collapse back into a moral reading of Kant's position, albeit one that is now directed towards questions of good institutional design rather than the substantive content of legal outputs.

2.2.3 Kant's Reconstructive Method

The inability of the two interpretative stances just outlined to do justice to the complexity of Kant's text should lead us to attempt a fresh start. In Section 1, we saw that Kant claims that there is a postulate of public right: political and legal institutions are not merely useful tools to meet typical human needs, still less are they arbitrary exercises of domination. Even thinking of them as the product of fulfilled moral obligations is inadequate. Instead, the postulate provides the grounds on which we can know that the law-like phenomena we apprehend through our senses are expressions of right. This is the methodological basis of the *Doctrine of Right*. Following Kant, we call the object the categorical imperative requires us to postulate the noumenal republic, or the pure idea of a state.[79] Its constitution is based on the innate right of individuals and

---

[78] Ripstein, *Force and Freedom*, 145–181. Ripstein notes the significance of practical postulates to Kant's argument in a valuable appendix to *Force and Freedom*. However, he treats them as 'application[s] of normative concepts to objects of appearance' (see 182) in the sense of the moral reading, thus failing to grasp fully their *epistemological* significance in relation to the cognition of social phenomena as legal. For further discussion, see P. Capps and J. Rivers, 'Kant's Postulate of Public Right and Contemporary Legal Theory' (2025, forthcoming).

[79] See CF Draft 19:609–10.

characterised by a separation of legislative, executive and judicial powers within sovereign states that have legal relations with other sovereign states and their citizens (6:354–5). This idea renders intelligible, from the perspective of pure practical reason, the legal phenomena familiar to Kant.

Part of the puzzlement of modern interpreters stems from the mistaken assumption that the discussions of various legal examples in the *Doctrine of Right* must be instances of the application of abstract moral norms to concrete sets of facts, either by way of critique or to derive ideal alternatives from first principles. But this is an overly simplistic and, indeed, modern rendition of Kant's method, a rendition that depends on a strict distinction between the 'fact' of law and the 'norm' of moral judgment. The complexity of the relationship between the ideal and the actual in Kant is raised in the opening words of the Preface in which Kant explains the need for a metaphysical system of right to be developed in parallel with the empirical variety of cases (6:205–6). Each has to respond to the other, and be considered in the light of the other, yet without collapsing the distinction. Later on, Kant distinguishes between the *pure idea* of a system of public right and its possible *instantiation* in actual human arrangements (6:338, 341). Moreover, his concept of the a priori is not simply ideal; it extends to the need for ideas to be actualisable precisely because the concept of right is directed towards legal practice. A marginal comment in a draft of the 'Conflict of the Faculties' establishes this point:

> It is only a concept of a completely pure state constitution, namely the idea of a republic, where all those entitled to vote together have all power (either distributively in a democracy or conjunctively in a republic): *Respublica . . . noumenon* oder *phaenomenon*. The latter has three forms but *respublica noumenon* is only one and the same . . . An absolute monarch can still govern in a republican manner without forfeiting his strength. (CF Draft 19:609–10)

So there is an important distinction between the pure idea of the state and possible phenomenal instantiations of it in various institutional forms.[80] At numerous points, Kant shows considerable sensitivity to the inescapable empirical constraints that apply to any possible realisation of right, and those practical constraints apply a priori precisely because they are inescapable. Thus, the *Doctrine of Right* moves (often in reflective rather than linear fashion) between the pure idea of the state as a republican system, a discussion of the extent to which legal rules and institutions are unavoidable in its practical instantiation, reinterpretation of existing legal practices in the light of the pure idea and critique of egregious incompatibilities. Rather than offering us a simple contrast between description and evaluation, or abstract norm and concrete application, Kant engages a variety

---

[80] Peter Unruh claims that he is the first among German commentators to recognise this point. See Unruh, *Die Herrschaft der Vernunft*, 90–127.

of contemporary laws and political institutions with considerable subtlety. Fundamentally, though, we should not lose sight of the fact that Kant's concern is methodological. He is telling us how to do public law, not setting out, in detail, what public law is. The *Doctrine of Right* is philosophical rather than doctrinal, which would be the proper preserve of the law professor.[81] This is the method of the postulate, and it can fairly be called non-positivist and reconstructive. In modern legal philosophy, it is closest to the interpretative method of theorists such as Habermas and Dworkin.[82]

2.3 The Three Powers

2.3.1 Legislative Power and the Location of Sovereignty

Kant's method is well illustrated by his discussion of legislative power. A state is a 'union of a multitude of human beings under laws of right' and is also called the 'concurring and united', or omnilateral [*allseitige*], will (6:259, 263). The pure idea of the state serves as a 'norm' for the internal constitution of every actual union and is given effect in an institutional structure comprising legislative, executive and judicial bodies (6:313). The distinction between powers was already familiar at the time Kant was writing, and it seems entirely routine. However, while Achenwall thought that the main powers of the state could be exercised by a single 'public overlord', Kant considered that these institutions are functionally distinct, and should not be combined in one person.[83]

Kant's views on the relationship between legislative, executive and judicial institutions took some time to settle. In his early notes on Achenwall, he writes the following:

> Majesty befits the one who is not subordinated; supreme power the one who is supreme among all subordinates. The government [*Regirung*] is under the laws and thus has no majesty. It is not holy for it can rightly be held responsible. The souverain cannot govern, for the regent stands under the laws, is obligated to rule in conformity with them, and can be held responsible. In contrast the law (*ex voluntate communi*) is beyond reproach and is holy. The *dignitas legislatoria* is thus *majestas* and the legislator is beyond reproach. . . . Yet in addition the judge can judge the government but not *valide*, and the *souverain* has *potestatem inspectoriam* [oversight powers] over both. (RPR 19:500)[84]

---

[81] See Capps and Rivers, 'Kant's Postulate of Public Right and Contemporary Legal Theory'.

[82] See: Habermas, *Between Facts and Norms*; Dworkin, *A Matter of Principle*, 146–166; *Law's Empire*, 55–62, 228–38; *Justice in Robes*, 1–35 and 223–240.

[83] Achenwall reflected older discussions, and an increasingly paternalistic German tradition, by identifying legislative, executive and 'oversight' powers. See his *Ius Naturae*, II, §§113–19. See also Guyer, 'Achenwall, Kant, and the Division of Governmental Powers', 207.

[84] See also TPP (8:352–3) where Kant commends Frederick the Great for saying that he was only the nation's highest servant of the state.

Here, the attribute of 'majesty' is associated with the 'dignity of legislation', and the legislature is 'sovereign'. It is easy to see the influence of Rousseau on this conception of legislative sovereignty. The legislator has oversight powers over the judiciary and executive; in addition, the executive must abide by the law and whether this has been done is to be determined by the judiciary (what he means by 'not *valide*' will be considered later).[85]

By the time that Kant wrote the *Doctrine of Right*, his view of legislative supremacy had been moderated by its location within a sovereign system of law:

> ... the three authorities in a state are, *first*, coordinate with one another (*postestates coordinatae*) as so many moral persons, that is, each complements the others to complete the constitution of a state (*complementum ad sufficientiam*). But, *second*, they are also subordinate (*subordinatae*) to one another, so that one of them, in assisting another, cannot also usurp its function; instead, each has its own principle, that is, it indeed commands in its capacity [*Qualität*] as a particular person still under the condition of the will of a superior. *Third*, though the union of both each subject is apportioned his rights. (6:316)[86]

The legislator is not uniquely supreme over the other two branches of government. Instead, the pure idea of a sovereign state comprises all three powers acting together, coordinate with, and subordinate to, each other. Each of the three 'authorities' has its own competence, and is supreme within its sphere:

> ... the will of the *legislator* (legislatoris) with regard to what is externally mine or yours is *irreproachable* (*irreprehensible*); that the executive power of the *supreme ruler* (*summi rectoris*) is *irresistible*; and that the verdict of the highest *judge* (*supremi iudicis*) is *irreversible* .... (6:316)

Since each power has its own distinctive supremacy, exercised by the highest organ within each branch of government, the legal power of each is limited. The legislature must not govern, and the government must not legislate. For Kant, combining the powers to legislate and execute is the essence of despotism (6:316–7; TPP 8:352). Nor may either the legislature or the executive power act as judge (6:317). At the same time, each is simultaneously under the will of another: the legislator can remove the executive but cannot coerce it; the executive can appoint judges but cannot sit in judgment on their deliberations; judges can only apply the law but cannot legislate or coerce. In short, each

---

[85] See 50–52.

[86] Gregor notes in her translation to the *Metaphysics of Morals* (note 26) that the text may be corrupted in this passage. We take the 'union of both' to refer to the combination of distinct competence and mutual subordination.

power can only fulfil its function with the help of the others, rather like the interacting parts of a clock.[87]

The challenges of putting such a pure model of separated powers into practice are evident. While still insisting on the supremacy of each institution in respect of its own function, Kant draws an analogy with the practical syllogism (6:313).[88] Legislation results in general laws, and these represent the major premise under which individual cases may be subsumed (6:313). Quite how the executive power correlates to the minor premise and the judiciary to the conclusion will be explored further in the next sections. The point for now is that sovereignty is represented most fully in the person of the legislator. This pre-eminence follows from the fact that legislation is the product of the '. . . the concurring and united will of all . . ., insofar as each decides the same thing for all and all for each' (6:314). Although the pure idea of sovereignty relates to the constitutional system as a whole, the 'sovereign' as a real embodied institution is the person or group who holds legislative power. There is both a temporal and a logical pre-eminence to legislation as the formation of general rules. This is not inconsistent; it is the only way of instantiating the pure idea of the state as an omnilateral will expressing itself through law.

In a pure republic, this legislative power would be exercised by all. However, in any actual republic, legislative power has to be exercised by all citizens acting through their delegates or deputies in a representative system (6:341). The need for representation means that the 'only qualification for being a citizen is being fit to vote' (6:314). At this point, Kant makes some comments that cause puzzlement and consternation in equal measure among modern readers. Women, minors, servants, hired labourers and private tutors are all mere 'underlings' or 'associates' of the commonwealth. They are passive and not active citizens – which is to say that they cannot act as legislators and they do not have the vote. Laws are made for them, but not by them.

Of course, like all of us, Kant was subject to the prejudices of his age. However, we need to remember his method if we are to read him fairly. His basic point – which is to say, his claim as to what follows a priori for any possible instantiation of the idea of public right – is that there must be a distinction between active and

---

[87] Kant does entertain some exceptional circumstances where there may be no choice but to allow an exception to the separation of powers. For example, in section E of his General Remark, he sets out what amounts to a sovereign prerogative of mercy (6:334). See also Fenve, *Late Kant*, 34–46. Elsewhere, he discusses the Millers Arnold Case with a degree of ambivalence we might not assume given his main claims about the separation of powers (CF Draft 19: 607). On the analogy of the state to a clock to describe the workings of the Prussian state at the time, see Koskenniemi, *To the Uttermost Parts of the Earth*, 797–870.

[88] Guyer (note 83, 218–19) observes that the practical syllogism was in use at the time, citing Georg Friedrich Meier.

passive citizens. Active citizenship depends upon the realisation of the idea of innate right. To be 'free' in law means that citizens must give consent to laws. To be 'equal' means that the system of lawmaking should not recognise '... among the *people* any superior with the moral capacity to bind him as a matter of right in a way that he could not in turn bind the other' (6:314). 'Civil *independence*' means that citizens owe their 'existence and preservation to [their] own rights and powers as members of the commonwealth, not to the choice of another among the people'. These three conditions together result in 'civil personality', which as far as lawmaking is concerned means that one does not need to be represented in the legislature by another – one could be a legislator oneself.

Although all human beings enjoy freedom, equality and independence as moral attributes simply by virtue of their humanity, not all human beings actually enjoy them in practice. Kant does not spend time speculating on whether the examples would be different under different social conditions, although he does distinguish between the 'blacksmith in India' who is a hired labourer, and a European independent craftsman (6:314–5). What concerns him is the need for voters and legislators to be active citizens, and the existence of an inescapable category of passive citizen. The alternative is legislation by those who are, in fact, dominated by others. And on this point, he is surely correct; some persons, such as young children, must inevitably be incapable of partici-pating actively in government. The obviously unpalatable examples Kant uses should not distract us from the necessity of the distinction, or the reforming implication that for an autocrat to legislate without taking the views of citizens into account is to treat them incorrectly as passive.

Thus, in his discussion of legislative sovereignty, Kant moves between the pure idea of a sovereign system of law, the practical supremacy of the legisla-ture, the inescapable need for representation and the distinction between active and passive citizens. These refinements emerge as he reflects on the inescapable consequences of instantiating the noumenal republic.

2.3.2 Executive Power and Subordination to Law

As we have seen, the noumenal republic gives the executive a coordinated role alongside the other branches of government, supreme in its coercive capacity. Yet the necessary instantiation of the pure idea of the state takes the form of a practical syllogism in which the executive branch is the minor premise, since it 'contains the command to behave in accordance with the law, that is, the principle of subsump-tion under the law' (6:314). At first sight, the analogy is puzzling, but the puzzle can be resolved once again by attending to his method. Up to this point of the book, Kant has been setting out the basic features of private right – the law of property, contract and domestic relations – and we might think that the role of the executive branch is strictly limited to enforcing judgments of courts in private litigation. We might then also think of the criminal justice system in which the executive branch has an additional role in bringing prosecutions as well as carrying out any punishment ordered by the court. But in neither case does the executive branch seem to figure *between* the law and the court's judgment. On the contrary, if adjudication takes the form of a practical syllogism, the minor premise seems to consist of the facts for determination by judge or jury. Once the facts have been settled, the law can be applied and the judgment as to what the law requires in the concrete case can be issued. If there is any 'command to behave in accordance with the law', it would seem to flow either from the law itself (the major premise) or the judge's order (the conclusion). What does he mean?

It is important to note that much of Kant's discussion of executive power is found in the General Remark, and thus his views may be more tentative or open. He would not deny the role of the executive in bringing prosecutions and punishing criminals. He says as much at the opening of section E of the General Remark (6:331) where he talks of the power of the ruler (*Befehlshaber*). He immediately repeats an earlier point that the highest ruler in the state cannot be punished (6:317). This follows straightforwardly from his claim that the distinguishing characteristic of the executive branch is its monopoly of coercion, and that the highest member of that branch (*Oberbefehlshaber*) cannot therefore be coerced (6:316). The sovereign (i.e. the legislator) can dismiss the ruler or reform the administration but cannot compel either. This separation of legislative and executive power is necessary to ensure that the executive branch remains subject to law and does not slide into despotism.

Kant defines the task of Government as appointing 'magistrates' – we might say public officials – and 'prescribing to the people rules in accordance with which each of them can acquire something or preserve what is his in accordance with the law (through subsumption of a case under it)' (6:316). The 'Regent', 'Government' or 'Directorate' issues directives (*Befehle*) to the public, and to the magistrates and ministers charged with state administration. These decrees are not laws; they are 'ordinances'. A little later he suggests that ordinances relate to particular cases and may be changed. This leads some commentators to suggest that the role of the executive Kant has in mind is primarily to regulate markets. An example would be the creation of a Land Registry to enable individuals to secure their property by registering its precise boundaries and their legal interest in a publicly accessible and reliable manner.[89]

---

[89] See e.g. Byrd and Hruschka, *Kant's 'Doctrine of Right'*, 155–61. See, more generally, Clarke, *Iron Kingdom*, 145–283 for examples during Frederick the Great's reforms of Prussian bureaucracy.

However, the clearest expression of Kant's assumptions about the role of the executive branch can be found in Section B of the General Remark (6:323–5). His basic point is that the powers of the Government derive from the people and should be exercised for public purposes. This leads him to reinterpret traditional conceptions of the monarch as 'supreme owner' (*Obereigentümer*) to mean 'supreme ruler' (*Oberbefehlshaber*). People are not external objects capable of belonging to rulers. He further relativises the idea of 'supreme ownership' by insisting that it is really only the idea of civil association designed to secure private ownership under public general laws. For this reason, the 'supreme ruler' should not have private estates; such a practice runs the risk of expanding into state ownership of property and turning people into serfs. For the same reason, he is also hostile to the idea of corporations or estates of the realm with perpetual succession (he instances military and clerical orders). Taxation must have the consent of the people; police powers provide for 'public security, convenience and decency', and the need to preserve the state leads to a right to inspect private associations and – in cases of necessity and with sufficient higher authority – a right to search private property. This is what it means to reimagine actual executive power in the light of the noumenal republic and not as the heritable possession of a monarch or ruling class.

Kant seems to imply that all these executive powers are necessarily implicit in the task of Government. In Section C, he discusses the 'indirect' duty to tax in order to preserve the people by providing the poor, orphans and churches (6:326–8). His idea here seems to be that although this is primarily a matter for personal provision in fulfilment of charitable and pious duties, the people collectively could resolve to authorise the Government to fulfil these duties on its behalf.[90] Kant was no libertarian opponent of the redistributive state.[91] Then in Section D he discusses appointments to salaried administrative positions and the distribution of dignities (6:328–30). All these examples provide us with a relatively straightforward answer to our opening puzzle. The most frequent characteristic action of the executive branch mentioned or implied by Kant is taxation. The model that he has in mind with the practical syllogism is neither private nor criminal law, in which the minor premise most naturally relates to the facts generating liability, but administrative law conceived as interferences with private rights that require statutory authorisation. The question in each case is whether the individualised 'command to comply with the law' really does have the legal warrant it claims. What is characteristic about executive power is, positively, the way in which it can reflect omnilateral consent for the pursuit of

---

[90] Legislation on imperfect duties can be consented to; see Rel (6:95–7).

[91] See also, Rosen, *Kant's Theory of Justice*; Kaufman, *Welfare in the Kantian State*.

public purposes and, negatively, the need for it to be exercised within the bounds of general law. The obviousness of such a claim to us today should not blind us to the extent of constructive reinterpretation Kant engages in to show how the idea of public right is expressed in the institutional arrangements of his day.

2.3.3 Judicial Power and Innate Right

Kant's view, that executive power has inevitably to be subordinated to law, is reinforced by the relationship between judicial power and innate right. Kant's short paragraph on the nature of judicial power (6:317) is best read against the background of a growing consensus among European constitutionalists about the importance of judicial independence in protecting natural rights against governmental encroachment. Accounts of the separation of powers in the seventeenth and early eighteenth centuries tended to focus on the overriding importance of separating legislative and executive power. Judges were typically seen as subordinate public officials, a mere sub-branch of the executive power, holding office for as long as it should please the monarch. However, as the eighteenth century progressed, an increasing number of natural right theorists argued that natural rights were preserved rather than relinquished on entering the civil condition, and judges took on a new significance as defenders of these natural rights within the law.[92] Montesquieu famously saw in the English jury a practical manifestation of the same spirit of liberty and a fundamental bulwark against executive oppression.[93]

Kant follows Achenwall in dividing natural right into innate right (quite literally, the right we are born with) and acquired rights to property, contract and domestic relations, which are brought about through natural acts of unified willing among human beings. Unlike Achenwall, Kant argues that there is only one innate right, which is multifaceted. Its most important feature is 'freedom':

> *Freedom* (independence from being constrained by another's choice), insofar as it can coexist with the freedom of every other in accordance with a universal law, is the only original right belonging to every man by virtue of his humanity. (6:237)

Innate right is thus a logical correlative of the duty each of us has to refrain from subordinating the will of others to our own, which in turn is an expression of duties contained in the Formula of the End in Itself (6:237, 230–1). It has four other features: equality, independence, innocence and relationality. We are naturally each other's equals in the sense that we need not be bound by others

---

[92] See Rivers, 'Natural Law, Human Rights and the Separation of Powers'.
[93] Montesquieu, *The Spirit of the Laws*, 156–166.

to more than we can in turn bind them. This means that we are our own masters ('*sui iuris*', the Latin term for an emancipated son). We are also beyond reproach in the sense that we start from a position of legal innocence until we do something to wrong another. The fifth and final feature of innate right is often overlooked but is of vital importance for Kant's understanding of the emergence of other acquired rights and, ultimately, the civil condition. This is 'the authorisation to do to others anything which does not in itself reduce what is theirs, so long as [i.e. even if] they do not want to accept it' (6:238). Kant instances speaking to another, and even telling a lie or making a false promise, since it is up to the other whether to take it seriously. Inducing reliance and causing loss is wrongful, as of course is physical contact without consent, but reaching out in friendship to another person is not wrongful, even if it should prove to be unwelcome. Indeed, it is only with the capacity to befriend others and explore the possible unification of our wills that we can conceive of a contract or a state coming into being. In short, Kant conceives of innate right as a single set of interrelated aspects of juridical personhood, with both formal and substantive implications.

We have already seen that innate right leads to the supremacy of legislation, which reflects the omnilateral will; it also leads Kant to identify a parallel and independent source of legitimacy within judicial process, offering a rational case for trial by jury.

> Finally, neither the head of state nor its ruler can *judge*, but can only appoint judges as magistrates. A people judges itself through those of its fellow citizens whom it designates as its representatives for this by a free choice and, indeed, designates especially for each act. For a verdict (a sentence) is an individual act of public justice (*iustitiae distributativae*) performed by an administrator of the state (a judge or court) upon a subject, that is, upon someone belonging to the people; and so this act is invested with no authority to assign (allot) to a subject what is his. Since each individual among a people is only passive in this relationship (to the authorities), if either the legislative or the executive authority were to decide in a controversial case what belongs to him, it might do him a wrong, since it would not be the people itself doing this and pronouncing a verdict of *guilty* or *not guilty* upon a fellow citizen. But once the facts in a lawsuit have been established, the court has judicial authority to apply the law, and to render to each what is his with the help of the executive authority. Hence only the *people* can give a judgment upon one of its members, although only indirectly, by means of representatives (the jury) whom it has delegated. (6:317–8)

The key to this paragraph is to recognise that Kant is distinguishing the respective roles of judge and jury. The first sentence refers to the judge, who is a magistrate appointed by the head of state or governor. The second sentence refers to the jury, which Kant conceives of as selected by the people from among the people for each individual case, not appointed by executive power. The third sentence refers to the role of the judge in pronouncing judgment. This is not the jury saying 'guilty' or 'not guilty', but the judge saying 'you are condemned' or 'you are free' as a result of the jury's factual conclusions. Kant refers clearly here to an act performed by a state administrator who has in themselves no authority to fulfil the task of public justice. But once the facts have been established by the jury, then authority to pronounce judgment has been granted and the coercive force of the state can be released.[94] He closes by noting the representative nature of juries.

The hardest part of this argument is to see why the legislative and executive powers, which after all represent the sovereign omnilateral will and its agent, have no authority in the individual case. Kant seems to think that legislative authorisation extends only to the making of general laws, and that a parallel form of representation is needed to apply the laws to concrete cases. The accused person can be taken to have authorised the law in general, but not its application to his own case. After all, judgment turns on the resolution of disputed facts – his concrete acts and states of mind – which legislation cannot determine. As an accused person, he risks being merely passive in relation to the application of the law, and Kant must be connecting this point to his discussion of active and passive citizenship a few paragraphs previously. But if the people also select a representative fact-determining body, and if the accused participates in the selection by exercising his right to object to jury members, then he is actively, albeit indirectly, involved in the exercise of judicial power as well. This additional procedural institutionalisation of innate right confers legitimacy on what would otherwise be an illegitimate exercise of power in the application of general rules to particular facts. The jury turns out to be not merely a pragmatic device for securing civil liberty but an institutional expression of the noumenal republic.

Innate right also relates substantively to judicial power by establishing evidential and argumentative presumptions:[95]

> . . . that when a dispute arises about an acquired right and the question comes up, on whom does the burden of proof (. . .) fall, either about a controversial fact, or, if this is settled, about a controversial right, someone who refuses to accept this obligation can appeal methodically to his innate right to freedom (which is now specified in its various relations), as if he were appealing to various bases for rights. (6:238)

---

[94] Byrd and Hruschka endorse an alternative view on this point, arguing that the jury establish the facts (minor premise) and the judge applies the law (conclusion), but this overlooks Kant's assumption that the jury also 'give judgment' by applying the law to the facts to reach a verdict. See Byrd and Hruschka, *Kant's 'Doctrine of Right'*, 164–7.

[95] Ripstein, *Force and Freedom*, 218.

Innate right establishes the normative starting point in any legal dispute; it tells us who needs to provide justification. For example, the one who assaults another needs to show legal warrant (assault is a violation of innate right), but the one who merely tells a lie does not (the other remains free not to believe it). As Kant explains in a footnote, certain lies do indeed harm the subject of the lie, and these require justification (6:238). In the case of assault, justification can obviously be provided by the legislature, as when police are authorised to use force to arrest a suspected criminal. Although the idea that innate right is presumptive is taken directly from Achenwall's treatment,[96] Kant removes it from the context of the natural state and relocates it within the practical operation of legal institutions, transforming its practical significance.[97] As a result, certain restrictions on a person's autonomy are justifiable if authorised by a general law, but not otherwise. Such a claim would be fully in accord with the position arrived at in the common law world by the 1760s, as Kant recognised in the draft of the 'Conflict of the Faculties'.[98] The presumptive role of innate right in legal reasoning also suggests that judges are under an obligation to interpret legislation where possible in accordance with innate right: *in dubio pro libertate*.[99]

Is innate right *only* presumptive within the noumenal republic? That is to say, can the content of innate right always be disposed of by the legislature, or are there any absolute limits, any aspects in which consent is irrelevant? Kant offers two arguments in support of the latter position. First, in the only other explicit use of the idea of innate right in the *Doctrine of Right*, Kant appeals to it to explain why utilitarian theories of punishment are immoral. A person must never be used as a means to their own or any other social end; criminals are to be punished because they have committed a crime in violation of the law and for no other reason (6:331).[100] This no longer seems presumptive: the legislature is simply prohibited from imposing punishment for rehabilitative or deterrent purposes. Second, innate right only confers a negative right not to be coerced without consent; it does not of itself warrant coercive action to remedy any wrong committed. It therefore makes sense to relate the absolute limits of legislative action to violations of 'inner morality' (6:371), that is duties to

---

[96] See *Ius Naturae*, I, §§290–4.

[97] The effect of Achenwall's placement was that the 'overlord' could freely dispose of innate and acquired rights. Achenwall was an 'abridgment theorist' of natural rights, not a conditional preservationist like Kant.

[98] CF Draft (19: 607). The point is noted by Jean Louis de Lolme ('the English Montesquieu') in his successful work on *The Constitution of England*, 251–2. It is possible that Kant read this work in translation, although there is no positive evidence to that effect.

[99] Statutory interpretation to favour innate right is quite distinct from the examples of the 'equitable' reworking of clear contractual obligations that Kant rejects (6:234–5).

[100] Kant talks here of 'innate personality', but as he earlier points out there is only one innate right that has several dimensions (see 6:237–9).

self, such as the 'enforcement of a religion', 'compulsion to unnatural sins', 'assassination' (RPR 19:594–5) and the giving of 'false testimony' (CPrR 5:30). Refusing to comply with such problematic legal duties is neither coercive toward others nor amenable to consent either personally or vicariously through the legislature. This leads to a fairly narrow set of limits based around what would destroy one's own agency. Clearly, each of us *could* consent to a range of prima facie wrongs, and so too can the legislature on our collective behalf.

2.3.4 The Internal Relationship between the Powers

So far, we have seen several examples of the way in which Kant uses the noumenal republic to highlight the significance of certain features of the state, and even reconstruct them according to a new conceptual scheme. The subordination of the executive to law and the preservation of a core of innate right in the civil condition lead naturally to the related question of judicial enforcement. Here, Kant's reflections are both more radical and more allusive.

When Kant discusses 'equity' in order to dismiss it as a source of positive law (6:234–5), he makes an exception for cases in which the judge is disposing of his own rights, 'as for example when the crown itself bears the damages that others have incurred in its service and for which they petition it to indemnify them'. Traditionally, such claims were seen as a matter of royal grace and not of right, but comments elsewhere strengthen the possibility that Kant conceives of administrative process as essentially legal and potentially also judicial. Tucked into Part A of his General Remark, he writes that:

> ... the sovereign has only rights against his subjects and so no duties (that he can be coerced to fulfil). – Moreover even if the organ of the sovereign, the *ruler*, proceeds contrary to law, for example, if he goes against the law of equality in assigning the burdens of the state in matters of taxation, recruiting, and so forth, subjects may indeed oppose this injustice by complaints (*gravamina*) but not by resistance. (6:319)

This is a critical passage. First, Kant asserts the immunity of the sovereign legislature as representative of the omnilateral will. Then he takes the view that complaints against the executive are justified if, for example, officials arbitrarily enforce the law against one group and not another. Finally, the use of the term *gravamina* is notable: it suggests a formal process of complaint made to a state institution, traditionally to the 'sovereign' in the sense of the monarch.[101] Such

---

[101] Achenwall defines *gravamen* (grievance) as a wrong that a superior does to his subject, but only discusses it in the context of master–servant relations. See his *Ius Naturae*, II, §76. In Kant's time, it was also used in the sense of a complaint against an organ of government. See Kümin and Würgler, 'Petitions, Gravamina and the Early Modern State', 39–60.

petitions could also be made to the legislature, which in Kant's view would certainly be entitled to intervene through the passing of new legislation or dismissing the 'ruler', which might in practice bring about the dismissal of an errant official.[102] Did Kant also conceive of a potential role for the judiciary in hearing formal complaints?

In his notes on Achenwall, Kant is clear that the judicial branch can pass judgment *in a sense* on the executive. He says that judgment can be passed, but not *valide*.[103] As he explains in the Introduction to the *Doctrine of Right*, the power of the judge to pass judgment on the acts of another can be distinguished from mere imputation by reference to validity or rightful force.

> Imputation (*imputatio*) in the moral sense is the judgment by which someone is regarded as the author (*causa libera*) of an action, which is then called a deed (*factum*) and stands under laws. If the judgment also carries with it the rightful consequences of this deed, it is an imputation having rightful force [*Rechtskraft*] (*imputatio iudiciaria s. valida*); otherwise it is merely an imputation appraising the deed (*imputatio diiudicatoria*). – The (natural or moral) person that is authorized to impute with rightful force is called a judge or a court (*iudex s. forum*). (6:227)

This is an important distinction. If a bystander witnesses an act of deliberate and unjustified killing, she is able to attribute the act to the agent and – knowing the law – judge that he is guilty of homicide. This is mere imputation; her judgment is 'dijudicatory', which is a term used both here and also in his lectures from Achenwall's textbook.[104] By contrast, when a judge or court attributes an act of homicide to a person, that attribution has a new effect in law: the executioner's axe falls accordingly. This is what is meant by a *valid* judgment. We must therefore read Kant as saying that judicial power has two dimensions, a dijudicatory, or appraising, dimension and a validity dimension of coercive legal effect. When he says that judges can judge the acts of the executive, but not validly, he means that they are reduced to the appraising, dijudicatory, dimension. This makes sense: the judge can require the executive to enforce its judgment against a citizen, but the executive cannot be expected to enforce a judgment against itself, as he explained in his discussion of the separation of powers.

From this perspective, the fact that Kant qualifies his claim in the General Remark that the sovereign can have no duties by the phrase 'that he can be coerced to fulfil' takes on a new significance. In treating the core judicial function as imputation and appraisal, Kant reflects the ideal supremacy of each power within its own sphere. It follows from this that the judicial power

---

[102] See 44. Guyer, note 83, 212 and 215.   [103] See 41.   [104] See L-NR 27:1337.

could at least provide declaratory relief not only against the executive branch, but also against the legislature.[105] The most obvious example of this would be a declaration that a particular law infringes the inalienable core of innate right. Nowhere does Kant say this directly, but the hint is sufficient. The idea that the power to issue a declaratory judgment in defence of fundamental rights is inherent in the judicial role is radical, even today.

2.4 Global Legal Order

The noumenal republic is not limited to the internal structure of the sovereign state; public right also requires the embedding of states within a global legal order. Many contemporary Kantian scholars think that Kant advocated some sort of world state, such as a federal state, with institutions similar to those of nation states, but with a division of competence between global and national levels. Elsewhere, we have argued that such views are mistaken, and that Kant actually defends a voluntary confederation resulting in an interstate system of international law.[106] However, even convinced supporters of such a 'confederal' interpretation of Kant's work can doubt whether Kant did not really harbour a secret longing for a world republic.[107] From what we have said so far, this may seem a possible conclusion from the application of his method. Kant might think that the ideal form of global legal order is an omnilateral will institutionalised as a state on a global level, but that such an idea is necessarily instantiated in a confederal substitute. In this section, we defend the view that, for Kant, the confederal model of global legal order is both conceptually necessary and practically realisable.

In §43 of the *Doctrine of Right*, Kant tells us that all three branches of public right (the right of a state, the right of nations and cosmopolitan right) are inextricably linked and would collapse if any element were missing (6:311; see also TPP 8:350 n). The context implies that he is thinking about the conceptual relationship between the three branches rather than the stability of particular and actual instances of states and their international relations. This is the same logical puzzle he draws attention to in the Second Definitive Article of *Perpetual Peace*: if all the states were to join together into one global superstate, there would no longer be a law of nations or *international* law (TPP 8:354). The key question for Kant is how to imagine a global constitution that preserves the integrity of sovereign nation states.

At one level, his answer seems straightforward enough. The purpose of his proposed 'league of nations' is not to meddle in each other's internal affairs but

---

[105] As indeed Grotius recognised. See his *The Rights of War and Peace*, 670–671.
[106] Capps and Rivers, 'Kant's Concept of International Law', 229–57.
[107] Caranti, *The Kantian Federation*.

to defend each other from external attack. It must 'involve no sovereign authority (as in a civil constitution)' (6:344); it must be capable of being 'renounced at any time', and so it must be renewed regularly; it is designed to avoid 'actual war'. A little later, he reiterates the point that the 'right to peace' includes the 'right to an alliance (confederation) of several states for their common defence against any external or internal attacks, but not a league for attacking others and adding to their own territory' (6:349). This right to join a defensive League of Nations is subsidiary to another 'original' one, which is the right of a people to form itself into a commonwealth (6:350). Even an unjust state (i.e. one that makes it a maxim to break its treaties) cannot be dissolved, although it can be put under pressure to adopt a less bellicose stance. In the penultimate paragraph of the section on the right of nations in the *Doctrine of Right*, we find that the *'permanent congress of states'* operates as a system of dispute settlement, although mediation can also be provided by third party states (6:350).

Kant expressly draws a contrast between the institutional arrangement he is proposing and the example of the United States. It is known that he discussed the disputes that led to the American Revolution with his friend Joseph Green (1729–1786).[108] Kant appears to reject some of the arguments by Hamilton, Madison and Jay found in the *Federalist Papers*, without direct reference to them.[109] For Jay, there were two principal defects with the pre-federal Confederation of American States. First, within the Confederation, states retained plenary jurisdiction over their citizens.[110] Second, the confederation lacked an executive coercive power.[111] Their proposed federation would remedy both these defects. Without it, a confederacy – or what they also called 'a league' – would be a 'simple alliance offensive and defensive', and would 'place us in a situation to be alternate friends and enemies of each other, as our jealousy and rivalships, nourished by the intrigues of foreign nations, should prescribe to us'.[112]

Kant appears to take direct aim at these supposed defects. His argument rests on the confederation consisting of states governed in the spirit of republicanism. In the *Federalist Papers*, Hamilton explains that it is the inability of states to act morally that justifies a federal executive power.[113] Kant disagrees and argues that we can expect republican states, or at least states governed in the spirit of republicanism, to do so (TPP 8:350–1). This is not to be misunderstood as an empirical claim. Rather, the moral duty on states to govern in the spirit of

---

[108] Kuehn, *Kant: A Biography*, 154–5.
[109] See Ossipow, 'Research Note: Kant's Perpetual Peace and Its Hidden Sources: A Textual Approach', 357–89.
[110] Madison, Hamilton and Jay, *The Federalist Papers*, 147.   [111] Ibid., 149.
[112] Ibid., 148–9.   [113] Ibid., 149.

republicanism *contains* the duty to have their international relations governed by law, and so they need not be compelled to comply (TPP 8:355–6).[114] The laws that govern the confederation are not the product of a 'cosmopolitan common entity under a sovereign', but are 'nonetheless a legal condition of federation according to a collectively agreed right of peoples' (*gemeinschaftlich verabredeten Völkerrecht*; TPP 8:311, our translation). In modern terms, Kant imagines an interstate system, in which the republican state is simultaneously a subject of international law and an administrator of it.

The confederal interpretation of Kant's ideal is implied by his account of state sovereignty. We have already seen that for Kant, each of the three powers in the state enjoys its own distinctive type of supremacy. No one has any right to override the legislature; as a lawmaker, it is irreproachable. There can be no global legislature.[115] The executive branch of a state is supposed to be irresistible; this is not compatible with a transfer of ultimate coercive power (i.e. control of the armed forces) to a supranational entity.[116] Judicial power is unappealable; this is not compatible with a world court overruling the judgments of national courts. It is hard to see how global institutions *could* be formed compatibly with the existence of sovereign nation states, even if these are the institutions of a global federation.

Kant's account of cosmopolitan right also reinforces this reading. Cosmopolitan right concerns the possibility of commerce between any persons on the planet. Kant understands 'commerce' in both the specific sense of contractual exchange and also a wider sense of interrelation between human beings, for example, in establishing domestic relations. Although he does not say so explicitly, it is clear that cosmopolitan right derives directly from innate right, which includes the right to seek to establish relations with others in any way that is not wrongful. Since the planet is a single continuous globe, all people exist in a community of possible interaction. The principal limit to the right to attempt to establish relations with anyone in the world lies in the wrongfulness of settlement without the consent of those who are already settled. This would require a 'specific contract' (6:353). And this leads Kant to draw a further distinction: between settlements that are so far away from anyone else that they are rightful appropriations of new territory and settlements that encroach on territories already occupied, even by nomadic tribes. This distinction underlies his critique of European colonialism.[117]

---

[114] See further Capps and Rivers, 'Kant's Concept of International Law', 229–57, 248.

[115] CF Draft 19:610: 'To me the concept of a limited state constitution appears to contain a contradiction: For then it would be only a part of the legislative power.'

[116] Caranti is helpfully clear on this point (note 107, 57–9).

[117] For a discussion, see Flikschuh and Ypi (eds.), *Kant and Colonialism*.

Cosmopolitan right is the only example of 'world law' that imposes obligations on individuals. If there were a world legislature within a global federal state, one would expect to find rather more. As we have already seen, innate right is defeasible in relation to legislation. But at the global level, innate right only operates directly in conferring on individuals the right to seek to engage each other peaceably – there is no legislature. The actual laws within which cosmopolitan right are expressed are the laws of individual sovereign states, harmonised with each other in respect of their treatment of friendly aliens. Cosmopolitan right aims at 'the possible union of all nations with a view to certain universal laws for their possible commerce' (6:352).

The institutions of the growing global confederation are therefore limited to those that assist the members of this unique league of nations to resolve their disputes amicably and agree harmonised laws for the regulation of interstate trading and other relationships, and are a category of law closest to what would now be called private international law. Those institutions can only be sustained voluntarily; in that sense, they are precarious. But as *an idea*, the confederation ('the right of nations') is locked into place by the right of a state and cosmopolitan right. No other account of global legal order satisfies the conceptual demands of the noumenal republic.

There is still a question as to how such a confederation might come into being. In §61 of the *Doctrine of Right*, Kant argues that a 'state made up of nations' (*Völkerstaat*) cannot, in practice, extend over vast regions of the globe, and so perpetual peace is an unachievable idea. The temptation is to read this as suggesting that a global federal state is ideal but impossible, treating the confederation as a second-best solution. But we should not be misled by the term 'state made up of nations'. Kant also describes it as a 'universal association of states'. It is not only a global federal state that is unrealistic; even a voluntary confederation would be a challenge to achieve on a global level. What Kant means by continual approximation in the form of a growing confederation is not the gradual increase of form and competences, but the gradual addition of neighbouring states to an ever-growing permanent congress. Kant's models here are the Greek Amphictyonic league (6:344) and the assembly of the States-General in The Hague (6:350).[118] As he says in *Perpetual Peace*, a powerful republic could form a focal point for such a development (TPP 8:356). Kant insists that this association remains 'a voluntary and precarious coalition of various states' precisely in order to

---

[118] Bederman suggests that the Greek amphictyonies have often been 'represented the most sophisticated complex of treaty relations, approaching even a level of real international organisation'. He considers this to be 'unquestionably an extravagant claim'. Bederman, *International Law in Antiquity*, 170. See also Hall, 'International Relations', 100 ff.

realise the idea of public right.[119] Thus, where such associations emerge, we should not be misled by any claims they may make as to their permanence and authority. In reality – that is, in the light of the noumenal republic – they remain voluntary and precarious.

2.5 Revolution and Reform

Kant's method is most obviously at work in his well-known rejection of a right to revolution. Given the existence of an ideal state, just described, we might think that actions that transform actual regimes, which are often unjust, so that they are closer to the noumenal republic would be justified. To some extent, this is correct: we have just seen that continual approximation to a global legal order to secure perpetual peace is a political principle and a moral duty. Yet Kant would resist any claim that all action in pursuit of the noumenal republic is justified. Even this way of putting it sometimes distorts his underlying concern, which is to establish how constitutional changes should be interpreted as potential expressions of right. That is, his interest is not, fundamentally, in the moral legitimacy of action to bring about constitutional change, but rather in the possibility of interpreting the accidents of politics as expressions of public right. A theory of legitimate processes of constitutional reform emerges as a side effect of that interest.

Kant's starting point is that we have no empirical record of the origins of law (6:318–9, 339–40); it may have come about through an original contract, but given human nature it is more likely to have been brought about by brute force. This does not matter. There is, for Kant, no threshold above which a legal system must rise in order to be treated as an expression of the omnilateral will. The omnilateral will may be represented by one person (an autocrat), a few people or many. His view appears to be that there is an inescapable practical need for political representation, since the idea of the sovereign omnilateral will is only a 'thought-entity' (6:338). It follows that where there is no other potential representative of the people, the autocratic legislator is the sovereign representative of the people and must act as such.

This claim reflects his understanding of the relationship between the ideal, the necessary and the empirical. The following passage makes his approach clear:

> The different forms of states are only the *letter* (*littera*) of the original legislation in the civil state, and they may therefore remain as long as they are taken, by old and long-standing custom (and so only subjectively), to belong necessarily to the machinery of the constitution. But the *spirit* of the

---

[119] A similar account can be offered of the 'negative surrogate' passage in TPP (8:357).

original contract (*anima pacti originarii*) involves an obligation on the part of the constituting authority to make the *kind of government* suited to the idea of the original contract. Accordingly, even if this cannot be done all at once, it is under obligation to change the kind of government gradually and continually so that it harmonizes *in its effect* with the only constitution that accords with right, that of a pure republic, in such a way that the old (empirical) statutory forms, which served merely to bring about the submission of the people, are replaced by the original (rational) form, the only form which makes *freedom* the principle and indeed the condition for any exercise of *coercion*, as is required by a rightful constitution of a state in the strict sense of the word. (6:341)

Kant seems to be claiming that there is a 'constituting authority', which has the power and the duty to change the 'kind of government', if not all at once at least by gradual means, such that it accords with the noumenal republic. Taken out of context, this might suggest that the people can form a reforming constitutive power above the three regular powers of the state. But the term used for 'kind of government' (*Regierungsart*) is significant. Kant consistently uses the '*Regier-*' word group to refer to executive power. The 'constituting authority' must therefore refer to the omnilateral will as brought to expression in the legislature, and the 'kind of government' to the executive branch. There is therefore no contradiction here with the immediately preceding claim that there is no higher representative of the idea of a sovereign than the currently existing legislature. The legislature cannot decide to change its basic form, say from an aristocracy to an autocracy or to a democracy, as if it had the free choice to determine this. 'The right of supreme legislation in a commonwealth is not an alienable right but the most personal of rights' (6:342). Like it or not, the currently existing legislature represents the omnilateral will, and there is no other body that can authorise any change to that situation. Legislative supremacy is perpetual; it does not extend to the power to abandon that responsibility.

If the sovereign cannot abdicate, still less can any individual or group of citizens deprive the supreme legislature of its power. To recognise any right to resist the sovereign would be to elevate the resister's unilateral will above that of others. They themselves would assume the mantle of the sovereign. Revolution 'overthrows all civil rightful relations and therefore all right'; it dissolves the state and returns to a condition that is 'wrong in the highest degree' (6:307). The revolutionary makes an egregious moral error for precisely this reason. It is morally prohibited to cross the chasm between one constitutional system to another, because that would require us to pass through the natural condition, which is completely non-rightful. Legislative supremacy sets limits to the legitimacy of radical constitutional change.

Yet as he immediately points out, it must be permissible for the sovereign to reform the existing constitution so that it accords better with the idea of the original contract.

> A change in a (defective) constitution, which may certainly be necessary at times, can therefore be carried out only through reform by the sovereign itself, but not by the people, and therefore not by revolution; and when such a change takes place this reform can affect only the executive authority, not the legislative. (6:321–2)

Although the legislature is entitled to reform the executive power, it is limited in its means to do so. This limitation flows from the executive's coercive supremacy. It is not possible to have more power than the supreme commander.

> ... the constitution cannot contain any article that would make it possible for there to be some authority in a state to resist the supreme commander in case he should violate a law of the constitution, and so limit him. For someone who is to limit the authority in a state must have even more power than he whom he limits, or at least as much power as he has . . .. (6:319)

For the legislature to coerce would be to combine its function with that of the executive, and this is the hallmark of despotism. Kant is entirely clear-sighted about the ways in which 'people who have a lively interest in positions for themselves and their families' might be tempted to behave. Any resistance has to be 'negative' not active (6:322).[120] By negative resistance, Kant means 'a *refusal* of the people (in parliament) to accede to every demand the government puts forth as necessary for administering the state'. In essence, this is a democratic right exercised by the legislator against the executive; indeed instances are a sign of health in the body politic, since they show that the people's representatives have not been corrupted by the Government's purchase of influence. Negative resistance in the legislature can be supplemented by judicial processes employing criminal law, administrative remedies and *gravamina* to hold public officials to account. In the case of public officials, these, too, must respect the coercive supremacy of the executive power and the lawmaking supremacy of the legislature.

However, Kant has not quite finished with the possibility of change to the legislature itself. Although the one holding supreme legislative power has no authority to divest himself of that representative capacity, he may do things that result in the displacement of his power. The noumenal republic is best expressed in a representative system of the people in which citizens are united and act through delegates or deputies. If any existing supreme legislature does

---

[120] See also his discussion concerning 'freedom of the pen' (TP 8:304).

something that results in the emergence of an institution that better reflects the idea of the noumenal republic, then that institutional arrangement has to be seen as the new representative of the omnilateral will. This is how Kant explains the French Revolution (6:341–2).[121] Louis XVI convened the Estates General to deal with the problem of overwhelming public debts. This body took on the authorisation of taxation and the control of government expenditure, thus becoming the legislature and resulting in the monarch's loss of sovereignty. This new institution does not have to hand back the reins of government; indeed, it has no authority to do so, for example, by entering into an agreement with the old sovereign representative. Like it or not, and quite possibly by accident, it is now the sovereign representative (6:323).

Kant's position on constitutional reform is therefore very subtle. Although there is no authority for any existing legislature to reform itself out of existence, it is always an open question which of the various political institutions present in a state is the sovereign representative. Since this question can only be answered by reference to the idea of a noumenal republic, there is a historical 'ratchet' that legitimises and reinforces tentative and accidental progressive changes, but lends no aid to retrogressive ones unless they are irreversible.[122] Given that an autocratic sovereign is under obligation to represent the omnilateral will, and should realise that he is surrounded by active citizens better able to represent that will, he ought to find some way of including them within the exercise of legislative authority. But this duty does not permit the existing supreme legislator to remove himself or be removed by the people. It also follows that if a revolution succeeds, our duty is to give 'honest obedience' to the new authority, whoever that might happen to be. Counter-revolution is as illegitimate as was the revolution it seeks to reverse.[123] This is the effect of postulating public right as an idea of pure practical reason.

2.6 Conclusion

Kant closes the *Doctrine of Right* insisting that establishing universal and lasting peace is 'the entire final end of the doctrine of right within the limits of mere reason' (6:355). This is what underlies the provisionality of private right and the moral duty to enter into a civil condition, as well as the requirement for states to enter into a global system of peaceful relations. We must act on the

---

[121] Kant's interpretation, which has not generally found much favour with modern readers, is ably discussed and defended by Maliks, *Kant and the French Revolution*.

[122] 'The legitimation of a pre-republican state's authority is rooted not in the past but in the future.' Ludwig, '"The Right of a State" in Immanuel Kant's Doctrine of Right', at 415.

[123] This also explains Kant's opposition to colonialism, which wrongfully seeks to justify the eradication of indigenous systems of government in the name of 'civilisation' (6:353).

basis of perpetual peace, and work incessantly toward the idea of 'a republican-ism of all states, together and separately' (6:354). But achieving this state of affairs is no simple matter. The postulate of public right sets limits on the means that may be adopted as well as the ends to be achieved. And it takes considerable insight to discern what within the tangled web of legal affairs is already an authentic expression of the noumenal republic, and what is merely a provisional stage in its incremental manifestation.

Afterword

In this Element, we have tried to do three things. We have traced Kant's long intellectual journey from his inherited tradition of natural law theory to a groundbreaking moral case for the republican constitution and, beyond that, to the claim that the pure republic exists as a noumenal object underneath, behind and within all systems of law. This is the postulate of public right. Then we considered how the two dominant modern approaches to Kant's philosophy of law obscure this project by drawing a stricter distinction between the morally inert fact of law and our moral obligations towards each other. By contrast, when one understands the nature of Kant's project in his late philosophy of law, many of the interpretative puzzles that have long vexed commentators dis-appear, or at least become amenable to resolution. In a way that is entirely recognisable to modern legal scholars, Kant is trying to *make sense* of the legal system he finds himself in as an empirical phenomenon that is genuinely – not merely hypothetically – normative. Finally, we considered how Kant's discus-sion of the substance of public right shows him developing a pure rational system of law, reconstructing existing legal arrangements as expressions of such a system, and imagining alternative, and better, instantiations.

What is striking about this reading is the way in which it tends to reduce the distance between Kant's own work and the interpretative approaches of leading modern philosophers of law. Non-positivist legal theorists such as Jürgen Habermas, Ronald Dworkin and Robert Alexy have often drunk deeply from the wells of Kantian philosophy, and in spite of their own readings of Kant's later work, which are dominated by mainstream modern positivist interpret-ations, they have worked their way back to positions that are much more authentically Kantian than they themselves realise. In this way, the postulate of public right turns out to be not only the interpretative key that modern commentators on Kant's practical philosophy are searching for, but also a bridge that takes us all the way from Kant's own project in the philosophy of law to the basis for a revitalised legal method today.

Kant himself saw the potential relevance of his philosophical position for legal method. A note found among his papers after his death reads as follows:

> Pure and statutory doctrine of right are differentiated from each other as rational from empirical. But because the latter without the former would be simply a mechanical collection that is really not an objective (derived from laws of reason) but a merely subjective one (proceeding from the choices of the supreme power) and hence in itself containing no right, so it is necessary to insert a special part of the **doctrine of right in general** between the two connecting them together as a transition from the pure doctrine of right **to a statutory doctrine of right in general**. Such a discipline, which would be presented at best simply episodically by the law professors, would be very useful for instructing a future administrator of the law about domestic need as a transition from the rational to the empirical and for judging the latter in conformity with reason, indeed it would be necessary for this (but admittedly only for the philosopher as theoretician); however, the practitioner whom he would advise to close this gap, without seeking the principles themselves in accordance with which to determine whether the statutory laws themselves would be right or at least should be right, stubbornly denies them, but also sees them as necessary as they constantly patch and transform their legislation. (OP 21:178)

Kant saw himself as establishing the philosophical foundations for the possibility of comprehensive legal knowledge. Professional lawyers are then required to restate and practise law in the spirit of these foundations.

As it happened, Kant's *Doctrine of Right* did come to have a considerable influence on the development of legal doctrinal scholarship. As Nigel Simmonds observes in this regard,

> The forms of doctrinal reasoning and analysis that compose both the treatise and the judgment can be understood as an attempt to fit each discrete rule into a coherent system of social interaction, practice and understanding. The propositions offered in such contexts can legitimately be offered as propositions of law precisely in so far as they move our understanding of each isolated rule or doctrine closer to the archetype of law, when that archetype is more fully understood.[124]

In making this claim about Kant's influence on legal doctrine, Simmonds admits that his work is 'still very imperfectly understood'. We have offered an account here, which makes sense of its influence and defends its continuing centrality to our understanding of law.

---

[124] Simmonds, *Law as a Moral Idea*, 167.

Abbreviations

Citations are taken from the *Akademie Ausgabe* of the works of Immanuel Kant, as these are generally included in the margins of translations (e.g. 6:307). All the quotations included in this text are drawn from the translations provided in the Cambridge Edition of the Works of Immanuel Kant, unless stated otherwise. Given the extensive citations to the *Metaphysics of Morals* (1797) (in *Practical Philosophy* (Cambridge, Cambridge University Press, 2012. Translated and edited by M. Gregor), 353–604), in what follows, we will not use the title of the work. For all the other works by Kant that we cite, we will use an abbreviation of the title (e.g. TPP 8:349 n).

APL 'M. Immanuel Kant's Announcement of the Programme of His Lectures for the Winter Semester 1765–1766' (1765) in *Theoretical Philosophy* (1755–1770) (Cambridge: Cambridge University Press, 2014. Translated and edited by D. Walford with R. Meerbote), 287–300.

Log-Bl 'The Blomberg Logic' in *Lectures on Logic* (Cambridge: Cambridge University Press, 1992. Translated and edited by J. M. Young), 1–424.

CB 'Conjectural Beginning of Human History' (1786) in *Anthropology, History and Education* (Cambridge: Cambridge University Press, 2007. Translated and edited by R. Louden and G. Zöller), 160–75.

CF *Conflict of the Faculties* (1798) in *Religion and Rational Theology* (Cambridge: Cambridge University Press, 2000. Translated by P. Guyer and E. Matthews and edited by P. Guyer), 233–328.

CF Draft 'Draft for Conflict of the Faculties' in *Lectures and Drafts on Political Philosophy* (Cambridge: Cambridge University Press, 2016. Translated by K. Westphal and edited by F. Rauscher), 359–67.

Eth-C Georg Ludwig Collins, 'Lecture Notes on Practical Philosophy' (Winter Semester 1784–1785) in *Lectures on Ethics* (Cambridge: Cambridge University Press, 1997. Translated by P. Heath and edited by P. Heath and J. Schneewind), 37–222.

Eth-V Johann Friedrich Vigilantius, 'Lecture Notes on Kant's Lectures on the Metaphysics of Morals' (1793) in *Lectures on Ethics* (Cambridge: Cambridge University Press, 1997. Translated and edited by P. Heath and J. Schneewind), 249–452.

CJ *Critique of the Power of Judgment* (Cambridge, Cambridge University Press, 2000. Translated by P. Guyer and E. Matthews and edited by P. Guyer).

Corr *Correspondence* (Cambridge, Cambridge University Press, 1999. Translated and edited by Arnulf Zweig).

CPrR *Critique of Practical Reason* in *Practical Philosophy* (Cambridge, Cambridge University Press, 2012. Translated and edited by M. Gregor), 133–272.

CPR *Critique of Pure Reason* (1781) (Cambridge: Cambridge University Press, 2013. Translated and edited by P. Guyer and A. Wood), 133–272.

G *Groundwork of the Metaphysics of Morals* (1785) in *Practical Philosophy* (Cambridge: Cambridge University Press, 2012. Translated and edited by M. Gregor), 37–108.

MFNS *Metaphysical Foundations of Natural Science* (1786) in *Theoretical Philosophy after 1781* (Cambridge: Cambridge University Press, 2002. Translated by H. Allison, P. Heath, G. Hatfield and M. Friedman and edited by H. Allison and P. Heath), 171–270.

Eth-Mr 'C.C. Mrongovius, Kant's Lectures on Baumgarten's Practical Philosophy (Winter Semester, 1784–1785) (1785) in *Lectures on Ethics* (Cambridge: Cambridge University Press, 1997. Translated by P. Heath and edited by P. Heath and J. Schneewind), 223–48.

NF *Notes and Fragments* (Cambridge: Cambridge University Press, 2005. Translated by C. Bowman and F. Rauscher and edited by Paul Guyer).

NL 'Notes on Logic', in *Notes and Fragments* (Cambridge: Cambridge University Press, 2005. Translated by C. Bowman and F. Rauscher and edited by Paul Guyer), 26–67.

NOFBS 'Notes on the *Observations on the Feeling of the Beautiful and the Sublime*' (1764–1765) in *Notes and Fragments* (Cambridge: Cambridge University Press, 2005. Translated by C. Bowman and F. Rauscher and edited by P. Guyer).

L-NR 'Notes on Kant's Lectures on Natural Right (Winter Semester 1784–5)' by Feyerabend (1784) in *Lectures and Drafts on Political Philosophy* (Cambridge: Cambridge University Press, 2016. Translated by K. Westphal and edited by F. Rauscher), 81–180.

OP *Opus Postumum* (1803, first published in 1936 and 1938) (Cambridge: Cambridge University Press, 1993. Translated by E Förster and M. Rosen and edited by E. Förster).

Rel *Religion Within the Boundaries of Mere Reason* (1793) in *Religion and Rational Theology* (Cambridge: Cambridge University Press, 1996. Translated and edited by A. Wood and G. di Giovanni), 39–216.

RPR *Reflections on the Philosophy of Right* (1776–1804) in *Lectures and Drafts on Political Philosophy* (Cambridge: Cambridge University Press, 2016. Translated by K. Westphal and edited by F. Rauscher), 3–72.

RTL 'On a Supposed Right to Lie from Philanthropy' (1797) in *Practical Philosophy* (Cambridge: Cambridge University Press, 2012. Translated and edited by M. Gregor), 605–16.

TP 'On the Common Saying: That may be Correct in Theory, but It Is of No Use in Practice' (1793) in *Practical Philosophy* (Cambridge: Cambridge University Press, 2012. Translated and edited by M. Gregor), 273–310.

TPP 'Perpetual Peace' (1795) in *Practical Philosophy* (Cambridge: Cambridge University Press, 2012. Translated and edited by M. Gregor), 311–52.

UNH 'Idea for a Universal History with a Cosmopolitan Aim' (1784) in *Anthropology, History and Education* (Cambridge: Cambridge University Press, 2007. Translated and edited by R. Louden and G. Zöller), 107–20.

WOT 'What does it mean to orient oneself in thinking?' (1786) in *Religion and Rational Theology* (Cambridge: Cambridge University Press, 1996. Translated and edited by A. Wood and G. di Giovanni), 1–18.

Bibliography

Achenwall G., *Natural Law: A Translation of the Textbook for Kant's Lectures on Legal and Political Philosophy* (5th ed. 1763), P. Kleingeld (ed.), C. Vermeulen (trans.) with an Introduction by P. Guyer (London: Bloomsbury, 2020).

Alexy R., *The Argument from Injustice* (Oxford: Clarendon Press, 2002).

Alexy R., 'Kant's Non-Positivistic Concept of Law' (2019) 24 *Kantian Review* 497–512.

Allison H., *Kant's Theory of Freedom and Kant's Conception of Freedom: A Developmental and Critical Analysis* (Cambridge: Cambridge University Press, 2020).

Arendt H., *Lectures on Kant's Political Philosophy* (Chicago, IL: University of Chicago Press, 1992).

Austin J., *The Province of Jurisprudence Determined* (1832), W. Rumble (ed.) (Cambridge: Cambridge University Press, 1995).

Bacin S., 'Kant's Lectures on Ethics and Baumgarten's Moral Philosophy', in L. Denis and O. Sensen (eds.), *Kant's Lectures on Ethics: A Critical Guide* (Cambridge: Cambridge University Press, 2014), 15–33.

Baumgarten I. and Kant I., *Baumgarten's Elements of First Practical Philosophy: A Critical Translation with Kant's Reflections on Moral Philosophy* (1760), C. Fugate and J. Hymes (trans.) (London: Bloomsbury Academic, 2020).

Bederman D., *International Law in Antiquity* (Cambridge: Cambridge University Press, 2001).

Bentham J., 'Nonsense upon Stilts or Pandora's Box Opened', in P. Schofield, C. Pease-Watkin and C. Blamires (eds.), *The Collected Works of Jeremy Bentham* (Oxford: Clarendon Press, 2002), 318–402.

Brown S., 'Has Kant a Philosophy of Law' (1962) 71 *The Philosophical Review* 33–48.

Burlamaqui J. J., *The Principles of Natural and Politic Law* (1747–8), T. Nugent (trans.) and P. Korkman (ed.) (Indianapolis, IN: Liberty Fund, 2006).

Byrd S. and Hruschka J., *Kant's 'Doctrine of Right': A Commentary* (Cambridge: Cambridge University Press, 2010).

Capps P. and Rivers J., 'Kant's Concept of International Law' (2010) 16 *Legal Theory* 229–57.

Capps P. and Rivers J., 'Kant's Concept of Law' (2018) 63 *American Journal of Jurisprudence* 259–94.

Capps P. and Rivers J., 'Kant's Postulate of Public Right and Contemporary Legal Theory' (2025, forthcoming).

Caranti L., *The Kantian Federation* (Cambridge: Cambridge University Press, 2022).

Cassirer E., *Rousseau, Kant, Goethe: Two Essays* (New York: Harper & Row, 1963).

Chignell A., 'Belief in Kant' (2007) 116 *The Philosophical Review* 323–60.

Clark C., *The Iron Kingdom* (London: Penguin, 2006).

de Lolme J. L. , *The Constitution of England* (4th ed. 1784), D. Lieberman (ed.) (Carmel, IN: Liberty Fund, 2007).

Dworkin R., *A Matter of Principle* (Cambridge, MA: Harvard University Press, 1985).

Dworkin R., *Law's Empire* (London: Fontana Press, 1986).

Dworkin R., *Justice in Robes* (Cambridge, MA: The Belknap Press, 2006).

Fenve P., *Late Kant: Towards Another Law of the Earth* (London: Routledge, 2003).

Flikschuh K. and Ypi L. (eds.), *Kant and Colonialism: Historical and Critical Perspectives* (Oxford: Oxford University Press, 2014).

Gregory M., 'Kant's *Naturrecht Feyerabend*, Achenwall and the Role of the State' (2021) 13 *Kant Yearbook* 49–71.

Grotius H., *The Rights of War and Peace*, R. Tuck (ed.) (Indianapolis: Liberty Fund, 2006).

Guyer P., '"Hobbes is of the opposite opinion" Kant and Hobbes on the Three Authorities in the State' (2012) 25 *Hobbes Studies* 91–119.

Guyer P., *Kant on Freedom, Law and Happiness* (Cambridge: Cambridge University Press, 2012).

Guyer P., 'Achenwall, Kant, and the Division of Governmental Powers', in M. Ruffing, A. Schlitte and G. Sadun Bordoni (eds.), *Kants Naturrecht Feyerabend* (Berlin: De Gruyter, 2020), 201–28.

Haakonssen K., 'German Natural Law', in M. Goldie and R. Wokler (eds.), *Cambridge History of Eighteenth-Century Philosophy* (Cambridge: Cambridge University Press, 2006), 251–90.

Habermas J., *Between Facts and Norms: Contributions to a Discourse Theory of Law and Democracy*, W. Rehg (trans.) (Cambridge, MA: MIT Press, 1988).

Hall J., 'International Relations', in P. Sabin, H. van Wees and M. Whitby (eds.), *The Cambridge History of Greek and Roman Warfare Volume 1* (Cambridge: Cambridge University Press, 2008), 87–107.

Hart H., *Essays on Bentham: Jurisprudence and Political Philosophy* (Oxford: Oxford University Press, 1982).

Hart H., *The Concept of Law* (3rd ed.) (Oxford: Clarendon Press, 2012).

Hochstrasser T. J., *Natural Law Theories in the Early Enlightenment* (Cambridge: Cambridge University Press, 2000).

Kaufman A., *Welfare in the Kantian State* (Oxford: Oxford University Press, 1999).

Kersting W., *Wohlgeordnete Freiheit* (2nd ed.) (Frankfurt a. Main: Suhrkamp, 2016).

Kelsen H., *Introduction to the Problems of Legal Theory* (1934) B. Litschewski Paulson and S. Paulson (trans.) (Oxford: Clarendon Press, 1997).

Koskenniemi M., *To the Uttermost Parts of the Earth: Legal Imagination and International Power 1300–1870* (Cambridge: Cambridge University Press, 2021).

Kramer M., *In Defence of Legal Positivism* (Oxford University Press: Oxford, 2003).

Kümin B. and Würgler A., 'Petitions, Gravamina and the Early Modern State: Local Influence on Central Legislation in England and Germany (Hesse)' (1997) 17 *Parliaments, Estates & Representation* 39–60.

Kuehn M., *Kant: Eine Biographie* (München: C. H. Beck, 2003).

Kuehn M., *Kant: A Biography* (Cambridge: Cambridge University Press, 2010).

Kuehn M., 'Collins: Kant's Proto-Critical Position', in L. Denis and O. Sensen (eds.), *Kant's Lectures on Ethics: A Critical Guide* (Cambridge: Cambridge University Press, 2014), 51–67.

Ladd J., *Metaphysical Elements of Justice* (London: MacMillan, 1965).

Locke J., *Two Treatises on Government* (1690), P. Laslett (ed.) (Cambridge: Cambridge University Press, 1988).

Ludwig B., '"The Right of a State" in Immanuel Kant's Doctrine of Right' (1990) 28 *Journal of the History of Philosophy* 403–15.

Ludwig B., *Kants Rechtslehre* (2nd ed.) (Hamburg: Felix Meiner, 2005).

Ludwig B., *Immanuel Kant, Metaphysische Anfangsgründe der Rechtslehre* (4th ed.) (Hamburg: Felix Meiner Verlag, 2018).

Madison J., Hamilton A. and Jay J., *The Federalist Papers* (1788) (London: Penguin, 1987).

Maliks R., *Kant and the French Revolution* (Cambridge: Cambridge University Press, 2022).

Manfred K., *Kant: Eine Biographie* (München: C. H. Beck, 2003).

Marx K., 'Difference between the Democritean and Epicurean Philosophy of Nature', in Jack Cohen, Maurice Comforth, Maurice Dobb, et al. (eds.) and Dirk J. Struik and Sally R. Struik (trans.), *Karl Marx Frederick Engels Collected Works Volume 1* (London: Lawrence and Wishart, 1975).

Montesquieu C., *The Spirit of the Laws*, A. Cohler, B. Miller and H. Stone (eds.) (Cambridge: Cambridge University Press, 1989).

Murphy M., *Natural Law in Jurisprudence and Politics* (Cambridge: Cambridge University Press, 2006).

O'Neill O., *Constructing Authorities: Reason, Politics and Interpretation in Kant's Philosophy* (Cambridge: Cambridge University Press, 2015).

O'Neill O., 'Kant and the Social Contract Tradition', in *Constructing Authorities: Reason, Politics and Interpretation in Kant's Philosophy* (Cambridge: Cambridge University Press, 2015), 170–85.

Neuhouser F., *Foundations of Hegel's Social Theory: Actualizing Freedom* (Cambridge, MA: Harvard University Press, 2000).

Ossipow W., 'Research Note: Kant's Perpetual Peace and Its Hidden Sources: A Textual Approach' (2008) 14 *Swiss Political Science Review* 357–89.

Pinkard T., *German Philosophy 1760–1860: The Legacy of Idealism* (Cambridge: Cambridge University Press, 2002).

Postema G., *Bentham and the Common Law Tradition* (Oxford: Clarendon Press, 1986).

Rauscher F., *Naturalism and Realism in Kant's Ethics* (Cambridge: Cambridge University Press, 2015).

Raz J., *The Authority of Law* (Oxford: Oxford University Press, 1979).

Raz J., 'The Purity of the Pure Theory' (1983) 37 *Revue Internationale de Philosophie* 442–59.

Ripstein A., *Force and Freedom: Kant's Legal and Political Philosophy* (Cambridge, MA: Harvard University Press, 2009).

Rivers J., 'Natural Law, Human Rights and the Separation of Powers', in T. Angier, I. T. Benson and M. D. Retter (eds.), *The Cambridge Handbook of Natural Law and Human Rights* (Cambridge: Cambridge University Press, 2023), 308–23.

Rosen A., *Kant's Theory of Justice* (Ithaca, NY: Cornell University Press, 1993).

Rousseau J. J., *Discourse on Political Economy* (1755), C. Betts (ed.) (Oxford: Oxford University Press, 1994).

Rousseau J. J., *The Social Contract* (1762), C. Betts (ed.) (Oxford: Oxford University Press, 1994).

Simmonds N., *Law as a Moral Idea* (Oxford: Oxford University Press, 2007).

Stolleis M., *Geschichte des öffentlichen Rechts in Deutschland*, Bd. I (1600–1800) (München: C. H. Beck, 2012).

Tierney B., *Liberty & Law: The Idea of Permissive Natural Law, 1100–1800* (Washington, DC: The Catholic University of America Press, 2014).

Timmermann J., 'Mrongovius II: A Supplement to the Groundwork', in L. Denis and O. Sensen (eds.), *Kant's Lectures on Ethics: A Critical Guide* (Cambridge: Cambridge University Press, 2014) 68–83.

Unruh P., *Die Herrschaft der Vernunft* (Baden-Baden: Nomos, 2016).

Vorländer K., *Immanuel Kant: Der Mann and das Werk* (Leipzig: Felix Meiner Verlag, 1924).

Waldron J., 'Kant's Legal Positivism' (1996) 109 *Harvard Law Review* 1535–66.

Warda A., *Immanuel Kant's Bücher* (Berlin: Martin Breslauer Verlag, 1922).

Waxman W., *Kant's Anatomy of the Intelligent Mind* (Oxford: Oxford University Press, 2014).

Westphal K., 'A Kantian Justification of Possession', in M. Timmons (ed.), *Kant's Metaphysics of Morals: Interpretive Essays* (Oxford: Oxford University Press, 2002), 89–110, ch. 4.

Willaschek M., 'Why the Doctrine of Right Does Not Belong in the Metaphysics of Morals' (1997) 5 *Jarbuch für Recht und Ethik* 205–27.

Cambridge Elements ☰

The Philosophy of Immanuel Kant

Desmond Hogan

Princeton University

Desmond Hogan joined the philosophy department at Princeton in 2004. His interests include Kant, Leibniz and German rationalism, early modern philosophy, and questions about causation and freedom. Recent work includes 'Kant on the Foreknowledge of Contingent Truths', *Res Philosophica* 91 (1) (2014); 'Kant's Theory of Divine and Secondary Causation', in Brandon Look (ed.) *Leibniz and Kant*, Oxford University Press (2021); 'Kant and the Character of Mathematical Inference', in Carl Posy and Ofra Rechter (eds.) *Kant's Philosophy of Mathematics Vol. I*, Cambridge University Press (2020).

Howard Williams

University of Cardiff

Howard Williams was appointed Honorary Distinguished Professor at the Department of Politics and International Relations, University of Cardiff in 2014. He is also Emeritus Professor in Political Theory at the Department of International Politics, Aberystwyth University, a member of the Coleg Cymraeg Cenedlaethol (Welsh-language national college) and a Fellow of the Learned Society of Wales. He is the author of *Marx* (1980); *Kant's Political Philosophy* (1983); *Concepts of Ideology* (1988); *Hegel, Heraclitus and Marx's Dialectic* (1989); *International Relations in Political Theory* (1992); *International Relations and the Limits of Political Theory* (1996); *Kant's Critique of Hobbes: Sovereignty and Cosmopolitanism* (2003); *Kant and the End of War* (2012) and is currently editor of the journal Kantian Review. He is writing a book on the Kantian legacy in political philosophy for a new series edited by Paul Guyer.

Allen Wood

Indiana University

Allen Wood is Ward W. and Priscilla B. Woods Professor Emeritus at Stanford University. He was a John S. Guggenheim Fellow at the Free University in Berlin, a National Endowment for the Humanities Fellow at the University of Bonn and Isaiah Berlin Visiting Professor at the University of Oxford. He is on the editorial board of eight philosophy journals, five book series and The Stanford Encyclopedia of Philosophy. Along with Paul Guyer, Professor Wood is co-editor of The Cambridge Edition of the Works of Immanuel Kant and translator of the Critique of Pure Reason. He is the author or editor of a number of other works, mainly on Kant, Hegel and Karl Marx. His most recently published books are *Fichte's Ethical Thought*, Oxford University Press (2016) and *Kant and Religion*, Cambridge University Press (2020). Wood is a member of the American Academy of Arts and Sciences.

About the Series

This Cambridge Elements series provides an extensive overview of Kant's philosophy and its impact upon philosophy and philosophers. Distinguished Kant specialists provide an up-to-date summary of the results of current research in their fields and give their own take on what they believe are the most significant debates influencing research, drawing original conclusions.

Cambridge Elements $\equiv$

The Philosophy of Immanuel Kant

Printed in the United States
by Baker & Taylor Publisher Services

Printed in the United States
by Baker & Taylor Publisher Services